THE MOST DARING RAID OF THE CIVIL WAR

The Great Locomotive Chase

GORDON L. ROTTMAN

ROSEN
PUBLISHING

New York

This edition published in 2011 by:

The Rosen Publishing Group, Inc.
29 East 21st Street
New York, NY 10010

Additional end matter copyright © 2011 by The Rosen Publishing Group, Inc.

Library of Congress Cataloging-in-Publication Data

Rottman, Gordon L.

The most daring raid of the Civil War: the great locomotive chase/Gordon L. Rottman.

    p. cm. — (The most daring raids in history)

Includes bibliographical references and index.

ISBN 978-1-4488-1870-9 (library binding)

1. Chattanooga Railroad Expedition, 1862—Juvenile literature. I. Title. II. Title: Great locomotive chase.

E473.55.R665 2009

973.7'31—dc22

2010030195

Manufactured in the United States of America

CPSIA Compliance Information: Batch #W11YA: For further information, contact Rosen Publishing, New York, New York, at 1-800-237-9932.

Copyright © 2009 Osprey Publishing Limited. First published in paperback by Osprey Publishing Limited.

CONTENTS

INTRODUCTION

The American Civil War, often described as the first "modern war," saw a great deal of mobile warfare over large regions, with much reliance placed on the nation's well-developed railroad system. Trains were used to move troops and supplies to the front, shuttle reinforcements, and evacuate casualties. In April 1862 Union forces in southern Tennessee conducted an offensive into Alabama to the south, eventually seizing Huntsville, and then striking northeastward to take Chattanooga, Tennessee, just over the state line from Georgia.

Chattanooga was linked to Atlanta, Georgia, to the south-southeast by a 138-mile-long (222 kilometer), single-track railroad over which reinforcements and supplies could be sent to the Confederate stronghold. To hamper rail reinforcement efforts, the Union command developed an audacious and unprecedented plan. Led by a freelance civilian spy, Kentuckian James Andrews, a party of 22 volunteer soldiers from three Ohio infantry regiments, plus another civilian volunteer, would disable the rail line. Andrews was a colorful and somewhat shady character who had previously smuggled quinine into the south for military and civilian use, also developing a reputation as a spy, playing both sides of the line. Nonetheless, the Union decided to trust him with this unorthodox mission. Wearing civilian clothes, the raiders traveled in groups cross-country to Chattanooga and then bought train tickets on the Western & Atlantic

The Fletcher House (later to become the Kennesaw House and still identified as such) where the raiders spent the night of April 11. Beyond it is the Marietta Railroad Station where the raiders boarded their target train in the morning. Today the Kennesaw House is the Marietta Museum of History and next door is the Marietta *Gone with the Wind* Museum. The track to Big Shanty runs to the right. (Allen Shoppe)

Railroad to Marietta, Georgia, traveling on the same rail line they intended to disable. They were armed with the cover story that they were from Kentucky and intended to join a Kentuckian unit serving with the Confederate Army. In Marietta the next day they would board the northbound train to retrace their previous night's route back to Chattanooga, only this time they would be running the train themselves. They intended to steal it, right from under the nose of a Confederate Army camp at Big Shanty.

On April 12, 1862, the revolver-armed raiders stole the Chattanooga-bound train— the *General*—after the crew and other passengers had disembarked for breakfast. Dropping the passenger cars, the Union raiders headed north, pursued by the highly agitated and hugely determined conductor, William Fuller. Thus began what, 88 miles (142 km) and six hours later, came to be known as the Great Locomotive Chase and was to go down in history as one of the most exciting events of the Civil War.

The Andrews Raid is commonly called the Great Locomotive Chase, owing to the popular 1956 Walt Disney movie of the same name; it is also referred to as Andrews' Wild Raid, the Railroad Raid of '62, the Chattanooga Railroad Expedition, and the Mitchel Raid, as the raid was launched by Brigadier General Ormsby Mitchel. In the South the raiders were simply known as the Engine Thieves or Train Stealers.

Even though the phrase was not then in use, the Andrews Raid shows how critical small details and events are to special operations missions, and that no matter how well-planned the action, it can still be drastically affected by unforeseen circumstances. It also demonstrates that planners and the leaders on the ground can make decisions based only on what they know, and that they cannot perceive or anticipate what the enemy will do or what other external factors and events will impinge on the best-laid plans.

In the spring of 2008, the author drove and explored on foot the entire route of the Great Locomotive Chase. Remarkably, many of the sites, the bridges, stations, and other places are still there and marked. One can get a close-up appreciation of the terrain, vegetation, and weather, and how this affected one of the most unique military operations of the Civil War.

The north end of the 1,447 foot-long (441 m) tunnel through Chetoogeta Mountain—Tunnel Hill. It was from this end of the tunnel that the *General* and *Texas* emerged on their high-speed run northward. The original tunnel is no longer in use and the rails have been removed, but the tunnel's length may be walked by foot. The enlarged 1928 tunnel to the left is still in use. (Author)

ORIGINS

In the spring of 1862, the War in the West was in full swing and Confederate forces had to man a disconnected defensive line stretching from Memphis, Tennessee in the southwest corner of the state alongside the Mississippi River, running eastward north of the Mississippi and Alabama state lines and curving northeast through Chattanooga, Tennessee, just north of the Georgia state line, then following the North Carolina state line, and eastward through southern Virginia to Richmond, the Confederacy's capital. Roughly paralleling the Confederate front lines was a railroad line, mostly operated by the Memphis & Charleston and Virginia & Tennessee railroads. These lines provided the rebel armies with arms, munitions, rations, and supplies, as well as allowing the evacuation of casualties. They also permitted the rapid movement of large numbers of troops to reinforce against Union attacks or to concentrate for their own attacks and forays into the North. The railroads were not just another means of transportation; they radically altered strategic planning and capabilities. An entirely new strategic and logistical thought process evolved during the course of the Civil War, which some senior officers grasped quickly, and others did not. It was no accident that many of the war's major battles were fought over rail centers and that the advance and withdrawal of forces ebbed and flowed along rail lines. This was especially so since the road systems were crude and highly vulnerable to rain, which thousands of marching feet, horses, wagons, and caissons churned into mud. The flooding of countless streams in rainy weather created further problems and increased the reliance on rail travel.

The nation's sprawling railroads gave the opposing armies a strategic capability for rapidly moving masses of troops and logistics. Both sides quickly appreciated and exploited their potential. Here Union troops are loaded on boxcar roofs, a cooler alternative than the stifling boxcars, which may have been full of supplies.

On the eve of the Civil War the United States possessed more rail mileage than the rest of the world combined. More than 1,000 miles (1,609 km) in length, the east–west

rail line was served by "trunk lines" running into the South connecting major commercial centers and seaports, into which flowed essential goods and materials delivered by blockade runners. The Confederacy's factories, armories, plants, and fields furnished, albeit sparsely, goods and food to keep the war going. There were few such lines though. In the mid-South there were only three lines heading south: one from Memphis to New Orleans, another from Corinth, Mississippi, to Mobile, Alabama, and the third from Chattanooga (a main rail center) to one of the South's most important rail centers, Atlanta, Georgia. From there lines ran south and east connecting to lines running through the Carolinas and into Virginia, a major theater of the war.

The single line that wound its way through the north Georgia hills from Chattanooga south to Atlanta was the Western & Atlantic Railroad of the State of Georgia (W&ARR); also known simply as the "State Road." This 138-mile (222 km) state-owned rail line was established on December 21, 1836. Construction began on July 4, 1837 to be completed in 1848, with the exception of the tunnel through the 1,040 foot (317 m) high Chetoogeta Mountain (tunnel grade 840 feet [256 m]). Passengers had to stagecoach around the mountain to board another train on the other side, while goods were transferred to freight wagons. In an undeniable engineering feat the 1,447 foot (441 m) tunnel, which became known as Tunnel Hill, was completed in October 1849, and the first train ran through on May 9, 1850. As with other Southern railroads it had a 5 foot (1.524 m) gauge—Northern railroads were 4 feet 8.5 inches (1.435 m), today's U.S. standard gauge. While the W&A had only a single-track main line, rather than the preferred two, there were sidings to allow trains to bypass one another. Kingston, a key midway station and railyard, had four sidings while many other stations had only one or two; smaller stations often had none.

Two spurs branched off the W&A. The shortest was the Etowah Railroad, built to serve the Cooper Iron Works, running 2.5 miles (4 km) eastward along the north side of the Etowah River. Its single hauling engine, the *Yonah*, would play an important role in the coming chase. The other spur was the Rome Railroad running from Kingston 14 miles (23 km) west to Rome, Georgia. This short line was chartered by the Memphis Branch Railroad and Steamboat Company of Georgia in 1839 and was often unofficially called the "Rome and Kingston RR." A branch line turning from the W&A at Dalton ran northeast, connecting to the East Tennessee & Virginia RR at Cleveland, Tennessee. However, this latter branch line played no role in the chase nor did the Rome RR.

The Civil War was the first war in which railroads played a pivotal role. This was understood very early, particularly by the North, and with it came the realization that disrupting rail lines, at the right place and time, would be beneficial to any Union offensive. Most of these lines were fragile, being only single track and crossing numerous rivers and streams on easily ignitable wooden bridges. However, these lines were operated by dedicated professionals, were well maintained, and had adequate maintenance facilities and sufficient locomotives and rolling stock, at least at the beginning of the war. At that time, the W&A had 46 locomotives, far fewer than the North; the South had less than half the track miles found in the North—9,800 miles (15,772 km) as opposed to 20,800 miles (33,474 km)—but for the most part she was fighting a strategic defense, with occasional forays into the North, and relied on internal lines of communications. The North, though, had vastly more rolling stock: 451,000 rail cars compared with the South's 19,000. By 1862 the heavily used lines were in poor condition and little replacement rail was available.

In early 1862 Generals Ulysses S. Grant (Army of the Tennessee) and Don Carlos Buell (Army of the Ohio) thrust out of Illinois and Indiana across western and central

WESTERN & ATLANTIC STATIONS AND RELATED SITES

Station/Site	Mile	Station/Site	Mile
		Adairsville	69
Atlanta	0	Calhoun	79
Vinings	8	*Oostanaula River*	*83*
Marietta	20	Resaca	84
Big Shanty	28	Tilton	90
Moon's Station	30	Dalton	99
Acworth	35	Tunnel Hill	107
Allatoona	40	Ringgold	115
Etowah River	*44*	*Chase ends*	*116.3*
Etowah[1]	45	Graysville	121
Cartersville	47	*Tennessee state line*	*125*
Cass Station	52	Chickamauga	126
Kingston[2]	59	Chattanooga	138

1 Etowah RR to Cooper Iron Works.
2 Rome RR spur.

Kentucky into eastern Tennessee. In central Tennessee Brig. Gen. Ormsby M. Mitchel split off from 1st Corps of the Army of the Ohio with his 3rd Division. Striking out of Nashville, Tennessee, he occupied Murfreesboro.

Mitchel was under pressure from Lincoln, as were all Union commanders in the West, to make a strategic impact and begin isolating segments of the Confederacy from one another. His focus would be on seizing Huntsville, Alabama, and then Chattanooga, Tennessee. Capturing Huntsville rail center would cut Atlanta off from the east-to-west running connected lines: East Tennessee & Georgia, East Tennessee & Virginia, and Virginia & Tennessee. All supplies and materials coming out of Georgia would have to be routed east and northeast through the Carolinas to Petersburg, Virginia, and then railed back west on the previously named lines. Not only would seizing this linchpin city of 4,000, Alabama's third largest, severely disrupt Confederate logistics, but it would provide a base to support the drive to Atlanta, an even more important objective.

Tennessee was a steadfastly loyal supporter of the Confederate cause, providing more troops to the war effort than any other state, with the exception of Virginia. However, thousands of Tennesseans also fought for the North and there were Northern sympathizers in the Chattanooga area and throughout eastern Tennessee.

In October 1861 a Tennessean, William B. Carter, proposed to Gen. George H. Thomas, then commanding an independent force in eastern Kentucky, that bridge-burning raids could be launched into eastern Tennessee. Working with a Capt. David Fry, Carter organized a ring of civilian saboteurs and struck on the night of November 8–9. The results were staggering in both effect and reaction. The volunteers burned nine bridges in northeast Alabama, northwest Georgia, and southeast Tennessee

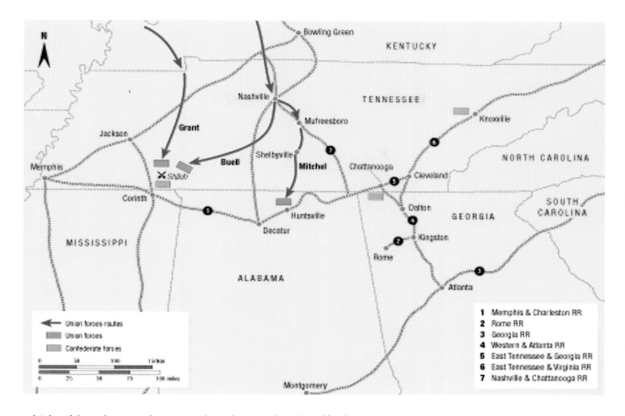

1 Memphis & Charleston RR
2 Rome RR
3 Georgia RR
4 Western & Atlanta RR
5 East Tennessee & Georgia RR
6 East Tennessee & Virginia RR
7 Nashville & Chattanooga RR

which, although not a large number, disrupted rail traffic for weeks. The most valuable effect, however, was that the raids sent shock waves through the Confederacy. The Rebel leadership was stunned and civilians realized with horror that there were insurgents in their midst. A counter-rebellion was under way and there was widespread fear that it might escalate, with direct attacks on loyal Southerners in their own homes. It was decided that this rebellion must be instantly crushed and any "bridge-burners" severely punished. The result was sweeping arrests of known Northern sympathizers and suspected insurrectionists. Brig. Gen. Danville Leadbetter was placed in command of troops responsible for guarding bridges and railroad facilities as well as rounding up bridge-burners. His efforts were heavy-handed and rapidly degenerated into a terror campaign. Many were arrested without sufficient legal grounds, and vigilante mobs lynched suspected insurgents found hiding in the hills, leaving them hanging beside bridges as examples.

In the long run these raids achieved little. Plans for a Northern offensive to exploit the initial success of the raids fell apart after disagreements among local commanders. Nor were any efforts made to destroy more bridges or impede their rebuilding. Another result of the bridge burnings was an outcry from eastern Tennessee Union loyalists begging for rescue from Southern tyranny and reprisals. Hundreds were jailed without trial, often simply to settle old scores.

Gen. Don Carlos Buell, Army of the Ohio, was charged by Lincoln to liberate eastern Tennessee. Buell dragged his feet and, irrespective of the President's wishes, focused more on central Tennessee, eventually taking Nashville in February. In March Buell was directly ordered to advance on Chattanooga, a mission he assigned to the more aggressive Mitchel's 10,000-man 3rd Division. The detached division marched

A typical Southern covered bridge, the primary target of Andrews' raiders. Covered bridges prolonged the life of the bridge and prevented winter icing.

through Murfreesboro and reached Shelbyville, positioning to attack Huntsville 200 miles (322 km) to the south and just across the Alabama state line. Mitchel's next intended objective would be Chattanooga, less than 200 miles to the northeast of Huntsville, advancing on the city's railroad axis. Chattanooga would be a tough nut to crack, especially if the Confederates were able to adequately reinforce and supply the rail center. It was protected by bands of high wooded ridges and hills on most sides, and a bend in the Tennessee River wrapped around the northwest side. Deep defensive positions were abundant and the avenues of approach were dominated by high ground. The maneuver of regiments on the thickly wooded and broken terrain would be extremely difficult. Mitchel was acutely aware of the Confederate ability to reinforce and supply Chattanooga from Atlanta via the W&A. This 136-mile-long (219 km) northwest Georgia rail line would become instrumental to both sides throughout 1864.

INITIAL STRATEGY

Brig. Gen. Ormsby M. Mitchel had graduated fifteenth from West Point in 1829, a classmate of Robert E. Lee. Deemed foolish and egotistic by some, he was, regardless, considered a genius by many others, having already made a name for himself as a mathematics professor, astronomer, attorney, and engineer—a true man for all seasons. "Old Stars," as he was known, had taken command of the Army of the Ohio's 3rd Division in September 1861 and was determined to establish a reputation by resolutely marching into Alabama, taking Huntsville and then Chattanooga, Tennessee, but he suffered frustration under Buell, whom he described as the "slowest person." Mitchel was very aware of the importance of the W&A line and the impact it could have on the coming Chattanooga campaign. The 3rd Division marched into Murfreesboro without resistance on March 21. Retreating rebels had burned three large railroad bridges, which took ten days to rebuild. To the rear the still-lagging Buell had yet to repair smaller bridges to allow supply trains forward. Mitchel requested that Buell grant him control of the railroad to facilitate his resupply and troop movements, but he never received this authority. The division sat waiting with little threat of Confederate attack until, finally, on March 27, Mitchel received vague orders from Buell to continue detached operations, but he still lacked control of the railroad. They marched on Shelbyville, Tennessee, 40 miles (64 km) to the southeast, to be greeted as liberators. In southwestern Tennessee Confederate forces rallied under Gen. Albert Sidney Johnson's smaller Army of Mississippi and launched a surprise attack on both Grant's and Buell's armies at Shiloh. The Battle of Shiloh (also known as Pittsburg Landing), one of the most bitterly fought battles of the war, took place on April 6–7 while the 3rd Division enjoyed a pleasant spring encampment on the Duck River 200 miles (322 km) to the east. Even though Union losses were higher in this, the most costly battle to date (13,000 to Johnson's 10,700), the North prevailed and Memphis was captured within weeks.

Someone had taken particular notice of the fact that the two bridges burned on the W&A line by the November bridge burners prevented any trains from arriving in Chattanooga for almost a week. This was the mysterious James Andrews, who had a reputation as a freelance "scout," then the "courteous" term for a spy. While not privileged to any degree of official access, he worked in the North as well as the Confederacy and was sometimes rumored to be a double agent. Andrews had developed numerous contacts in the South and also read the Southern papers—an important source of information, as armies on both sides had difficulty controlling

Brig. Gen. Ormsby M. Mitchel ("Old Stars"), commanding general of the 3rd Division, 1st Corps, Army of the Ohio. It was this aggressive and insistent general who supported and launched the Andrews Raid.

THE MYSTERIOUS JAMES J. ANDREWS

James Andrews was widely considered a man of mystery in his lifetime and there are still questions regarding his short life today—even his middle name is not known. It is believed that he was born in 1829 in Holliday's Cove, Virginia (today Weirton, West Virginia). Nothing is known of his youth until 1859, when he appeared in Flemingsburg, Kentucky, and took on odd jobs before finally becoming a house painter and singing teacher. Handsome, amiable, and possessed of a pleasant singing voice, he was known as a ladies' man, described by some as sociable but with few close friends. Nonetheless it is said that by the time of the Civil War he was engaged to an Elizabeth Layton. His political views he kept mostly to himself, other than that he believed in the restoration of the Union, and he did not have any known military experience.

In 1861 he quietly traveled south and developed a lucrative trade in smuggling quinine (scarce in the South and necessary to treat malaria) and other contraband, mostly notions (needles, pins, thread, buttons) and hardware. He apparently used his smuggling efforts to develop trust among his Southern contacts and quietly collected information on Confederate activities, dispositions, and so forth, which he duly reported back to Federal forces. Even common rankers had heard stories of Andrews the "spy" or "scout" working both sides. Many thought he was a Southern citizen taking advantage of the Union army for self-serving purposes—there were a number of such shady line crossers passing freely back and forth. Andrews had also developed connections and trust among Federal commanders in Tennessee, even though some saw him as a freelance double agent for sale to the highest bidder. Regardless of his questionable loyalties, he proved otherwise by proposing and leading a failed train-stealing, bridge-burning raid into Georgia in March 1862. As harrowing as the unsuccessful raid was, Andrews was not discouraged from making another attempt the following month, putting his life on the line once again. Whether he did it for the Union, glory, or profit, he was undoubtedly willing to take the risks. The 33-year old adventurer is generally described as 6 feet (183 cm) tall, about 185 pounds (84 kilograms), with gray eyes, thick black hair, and a short curling beard. He typically carried a .44 Henry Winchester rifle, although he did not take this on the raid. Fellow raider "Alf" Wilson described Andrews' demeanor: "He was a man who combined intelligence and refinement with cool dauntless courage that quailed under no difficulty or danger. He was a man deliberate in speech and calm in manner—a man fitted for the dangerous service he was engaged in, though I doubt his entire fitness to command men in sudden and unexpected emergencies. However, he shared his chances equally with us..."

James Andrews was eventually executed as a result of his raiding activities on June 7, 1862. He was buried at 3rd and Juniper Streets, NE, in Atlanta, and reburied in the National Cemetery, Chattanooga, Tennessee, on October 16, 1887, alongside the other executed raiders.

and limiting what the papers published. While not a military man, he was able to see the benefits of the destruction of railroad bridges and how this could be of advantage if coordinated with a Union offensive to take Huntsville and Chattanooga.

Andrews arrived at the 3rd Division's Shelbyville encampment the night of the Shiloh battle, April 6, and requested to speak to Gen. Mitchel. Little is known of the relationship or any previous arrangements between Mitchel and Andrews, although they had concocted an earlier unsuccessful train-stealing, bridge-burning expedition. There are no known written records or orders showing dealings between the two men. Neither would survive long enough to write memoirs.[1] It is likely that Andrews had already passed on valuable and verifiable intelligence information to Mitchel, otherwise the general would not have had the confidence and trust even to consider what he was about to propose. It is known that Andrews had previously offered his services to Gen. Buell, who had taken him up on the offer and sanctioned Andrews' proposal for an earlier behind-the-lines raid and turned him over to Mitchel for that attempt. He also provided intelligence information to Buell. After the war, Buell derided the raid and cast doubt on Andrews' value as an agent, claiming his information was mostly useless and out of date, and that his loyalty and reliability were questionable. This is thought to be an effort on Buell's part to sever any ties to the raid, which he felt was ill-conceived, poorly planned, and shabbily executed. It is doubtful that this was truly Buell's opinion at the time of his dealings with Andrews. Northern commanders were hungry for information from the South, Southern intentions and capabilities, and ideas that would assist their efforts to defeat the Confederacy. Regardless of the real value they may have provided, many more traditionally minded officers took a dim view of employing "scouts" and "line crossers." They held these shadowy individuals in no higher regard than they did the equally "unsavory" partisans, guerrillas, and bushwhackers.

Andrews had proposed to Buell a follow-up to November's poorly developed and coordinated bridge-burning raid, and it was passed to Mitchel. This one was to be coordinated with Union actions and would not be simply widespread random bridge-burnings without a definite objective—Mitchel liked precision, order, and coordination. He had planned his own bridge-burning campaign in Knoxville, Kentucky, the previous September, but the plan had been foiled by Brig. Gen. Sherman, who refused to allow Mitchel's division to march through his area.

Andrews's first attempted raid with Buell's approval occurred in late March. Andrews took eight men, volunteer soldiers of the 2nd Ohio Infantry, to Atlanta. There is no record of who these men were (bar one), their route, or the degree of support provided by Buell. One, though, was a relative of Corporal Pittenger, himself a future raider. This Private Frank Miller described to Pittenger how they had exchanged their blues for civilian garb and had taken four days to infiltrate through Confederate lines by road to Chattanooga. From there they took a W&A train to Atlanta and spent three days staying in different hotels. He told of the cover story they used to explain their presence; they were Kentuckians seeking to join a unit fighting for the South. Miller also discussed the annoyance of having to pretend to agree with the Southern cause, praise Southern leaders, and criticize Yankees. The plan relied on a turncoat W&A engineer assisting with seizing a northbound train, however the treacherous engineer was a no-show. As they waited, Andrews made discreet enquiries and found the engineer had been transferred to the Mobile & Ohio RR to help run troops northward, as the Battle of Shiloh was about to commence. Andrews considered stealing the train without the benefit of the engineer and asked if any of

---

1 Gen. Mitchel died of yellow fever October 30, 1862.

the men could run a locomotive. None could and he learned a valuable lesson. Heavy rains also hampered the effort. The plan had been to burn bridges, dislodge rails, and cut telegraph wires as the stolen train ran north, but Andrews was forced to release the men from the mission without achieving any of these objectives. The raiding party had no choice but to make their own way back to Union lines, no doubt facing difficult questions the farther north they traveled. All the men eventually returned, rattled but safe, and Miller would later recount that he considered himself fortunate to be alive.

This stillborn mission proved to be a beneficial dry run for Andrews. Undaunted, he remained in Georgia, considered the difficulties he encountered, and developed a more ambitious plan. In all probability he made additional trips up the W&A line to determine the most favorable station from which to steal a train, the locations of troops, and which stations had telegraphs; he would have studied train schedules and learned the intricate working of the rail junctions at Kingston, Dalton, and Chattanooga, which they would have to negotiate. In addition, he found the locations of woodyards and water tanks, timed the actions of his planned raid, and studied his primary targets—the bridges. The two longest bridges crossed the Etowah and Oostanaula rivers.[2] In total, eleven covered wooden bridges crossed the winding Chickamauga Creek and its branches. These covered bridges were mostly of the truss type, relatively short, and thus reasonably quick to repair. The roofed and sided housing cover was intended to protect the heavy and expensive wooden timbers from the weather. An unprotected wooden bridge might last nine years, but covered bridges could last many decades. The cover also helped prevent ice from forming by keeping the rails dry as winter winds rushed beneath the bridge. The most effective targets would be the lengthy Etowah and Oostanaula river bridges. These were timber truss bridges resting on high stone pillars and abutments, with the latter covered. In all there were 17 bridges on the W&A. Andrews also coordinated and gained support of local contacts he had developed, but no information exists about who these people were or the extent of aid they may have provided.

The meeting ran late into the night as Mitchel and staff officers listened to Andrews, studied maps, considered options, worked out details, and integrated the timing into the coming advance into Alabama and then on to Chattanooga. Once the details were worked out and an agreement was made, funds were provided and manpower was made available to Andrews. There was little time to gather the men, make preparations, infiltrate overland to Chattanooga, and travel to Marietta. It was already the night of Sunday, April 6; the train was to be stolen on the morning of Friday the 11th, and the raiders had to be in Marietta no later than the evening before.

It had begun to rain on the day of the meeting. It would rain for the next ten days, and this would have a major impact on the raid and Mitchel's advance. The high day temperature would be in the 80°F (27° C) range and the night low temperature in the upper 30°F (-10°C) range. Winds were generally light, but with occasional gusts, and the skies were overcast. Sunrise was about 7:00 AM and sunset at 5:30 PM.

The north Georgia hills are densely covered by elm, buckeye, poplar, hickory, maple, ash, elm, sweet gum, and various pines and oaks with a generally thick underbrush. The terrain is gently rolling and becomes higher and steeper the farther north one goes. Rivers and streams were slow flowing, usually with steep banks. The limited road system was crude, and cross-country movement through the wooded hills and ridges was extremely difficult as the raiders would learn, and the rain did not help.

---

2 Many northern Georgia place names bear Cherokee and other Native American names.

THE PLAN

As already detailed, Andrews proposed his bold and much improved plan to Mitchel on April 6. Andrews had obviously chosen to make his proposal to Mitchel in preference to the foot-dragging Buell. He may also have thought that the dynamic and forward-leaning Mitchel would be more receptive and supportive of an unconventional strategy. Mitchel was in a hurry to make a name for himself, and the engineer, mathematician, and astronomer in him were drawn to such a plan. He liked the idea of coordinated action between the raiders and his division and, if successful, the unconventional effort would be extremely valuable in supporting his advance—it just might open the door to Chattanooga and contribute to shortening the bloody war.

Andrews proposed leading two dozen men, recommended for their steadfastness by their commanders, to Chattanooga after infiltrating over 70 miles (113 km) by foot, horse, or wagon disguised as civilians. Fortunately there were no passport systems or travel restrictions in the area. From Chattanooga they would take a W&A train to Marietta only 12 miles (19 km) north of Atlanta in the heart of Georgia; it appears Andrews had decided that it would be safer to await the train in a smaller town than run the risks of Atlanta. To reach Marietta they would travel south on the same rail line along which they would later withdraw. They would stay overnight at hotels in Marietta on the night of April 10 to board the Chattanooga-bound train at 5:00 AM on the 11th. A cover story would be provided, with the men responding to any queries about their business that they were from Kentucky and were en route to enlist in a Kentuckian unit fighting for the South (Kentucky was another border state with mixed alliances)—this would explain their Midwestern accents. They had just four full days to plan and organize the mission, select the men and ready them, and infiltrate to Marietta in poor weather. It's likely that when Andrews approached Mitchel he had no inkling of how soon the fiery little general was going to move. If he had arrived a day later Mitchel and even Andrews himself may have deemed it too late to launch the raid in support of the upcoming advance. There was not a moment to lose.

The train they boarded would be stolen at Big Shanty, 8 miles (13 km) north of Marietta. Andrews had picked this station with great care. Big Shanty (renamed

The Georgia Western & Atlanta Railroad Station in Atlanta, the start point for the *General*'s morning run to Chattanooga, Tennessee. The *General* was the target of Andrews's "locomotive thieves." Confederate troops are loaded atop the string of boxcars.

Kennesaw in 1887) was merely a stopping place where the train would halt for breakfast at the W&A-built Lacy Hotel. There was no town, just the hotel, which doubled as the station, post office, and a few scattered dwellings. Andrews knew that at this stop the crew and passengers all unloaded for a quick breakfast, providing the ideal opportunity to seize the train unopposed. The other advantage of taking over the train at this location was that there was no telegraph station. However, directly across the tracks from the hotel was Camp McDonald.

Camp McDonald was opened in June 1861 and operated by the Georgia Military Institute in Marietta (an institution modeled after West Point). It served as a school for the 4th Brigade of Georgia Volunteers (Phillip's Legion), the instruction being provided by the facility and cadets of the institute. Briefly closed in the late fall of that year after the training cycle was completed, it reopened in early 1862 to train six newly raised regiments. It would close for good in 1863. The institute's presence appears to have lent a false sense of security to the train crew, resulting in few concerns about their leaving the train unattended for breakfast. Andrews, having already traveled the line on this particular run several times, was well aware of their schedule and the routine at Camp McDonald. Reveille at the camp was 6:00 AM, not long after the train arrived. The awakening troops would be cleaning up and preparing for morning formation while the train was unattended. Many of the guards were armed with unloaded muskets with fixed bayonets or 6 foot (1.8 m) pikes—known as "Joe Brown pikes," as they were advocated by the governor of the same name, who was overimpressed with their low cost compared with rifles, and envisioned them able to halt mass infantry and cavalry charges. Both rifles and pikes would be relatively ineffective in the hands of green recruits against determined men armed with revolvers, and equally poor for stopping a wayward train. Nonetheless, it would still be unnerving for the raiders to undertake such a bold move with a large body of troops so near at hand, even if they were still rubbing sleep from their eyes and looking forward to their breakfast of "peanut coffee" (parched and roasted peanuts, rye, and cow peas) and cornbread.

There were two parallel sidings on the west side of the main line. If any unscheduled trains came in from the north—a common occurrence because of military needs—the intended stolen train would not be blocked. The unscheduled train could be shuttled on to a siding to allow the regular freight or passenger train to proceed north on schedule, or the southbound train could pass on through if the regular train was not yet ready after its breakfast stop.

Andrews' assessment of his mediocre raiding attempt in March allowed him to improve and develop a more effective plan. He added more manpower to provide sufficient firepower if necessary, and recruited experienced engineers, to include backups in event of casualties, rather than relying on Southern turncoats. He may also have decided that, even though a smaller group would be less conspicuous when traveling, a larger group would be more resilient in a fight if casualties were suffered or some men simply abandoned the effort. Other than Camp McDonald there were no regular military units along the route, but there were local part-time militia and armed civilians who vividly recalled the November bridge-burnings. They would be more than willing to pursue train-stealers. The increased manpower was a wise decision; on that fateful morning four men failed to make the Marietta rendezvous, one of them the most experienced of the three engineers.

Andrews' plan was for his men to step off the train and give the impression that they were simply stretching their legs as the crew and passengers went into the hotel for breakfast. He would then discreetly move toward the head of the train on its right side, the side opposite the hotel, but in plain sight of the camp. They would uncouple the passenger cars, some men would board a boxcar while designated brakemen simultaneously climbed atop the boxcars. Andrews and his engineers would then board the locomotive, and be on their way. They would need to be done as soon as possible after arrival so that the locomotive's steam was still up; the less time spent there reduced any unexpected changes in events or the risk of attracting attention owing to any suspicious behavior.

Once out of sight they would stop and cut the telegraph line and the track to preclude pursuit. Even though there was no telegraph in Big Shanty, cutting the line was a wise precaution. As they sped north, stationmasters might become suspicious and telegraph enquiries back down the line. The raiders would head north at high speed, periodically cutting the telegraph line in case it was rapidly repaired farther down the line, as well as cutting the track. This would be accomplished by prying up rails. No demolitions would be involved.[3] Andrews did not plan on burning any of the smaller bridges until he reached the Etowah River and its big bridge, and then the Oostanaula River Bridge—both high-value targets. The bridges had to be burned south of Dalton as there was a branch line that ran northeast to connect to the same east–west line that the W&A connected to in Chattanooga.

Andrews was armed with an explanation to deceive stationmasters as they headed north. He would say they were on special assignment hauling gunpowder to Corinth in northern Mississippi for Gen. P.G.T. Beauregard, whose forces were currently in the area. He expected that word of the Union advance designed to coordinate with the raid would have been received by then. It was entirely possible, however, that their cover story would be questioned, because it was known the Yankees had cut the east–west line at Huntsville; Corinth was farther west. Additionally, none of the locomotive's crew would be recognized by stationmasters and yard workers: specific locomotives were assigned to particular runs with regular engineers and firemen. Thus the raid's increased manpower could be crucial if they needed to shoot their way out of a dire situation. This was unlikely though, as few, if any, W&A employees were armed, and there were apparently no armed guards at yards and stations. In fact, even after the November bridge-burnings and the increased security measures, there is no mention in contemporary writings of encountering bridge guards. Andrews' biggest fear was being shuttled to a siding to make way for unscheduled high-priority trains. Cutting the telegraph lines to the south prevented word of any unscheduled trains being sent ahead so they would have no advance warning if this was likely.

They would need to take on water and wood en route. Atlanta to Chattanooga was known as a "five-cord run," which meant at least two wood and watering stops. The tender carried only one and three-quarter cords of wood and the engine would be running at higher than normal speed.[4]

Assuming no unexpected difficulties, on reaching Chattanooga they would turn west at the Market Street crossing on to the Nashville & Chattanooga line then the Memphis & Charleston, and soon run into the advancing 3rd Division, moving east to take Chattanooga. No doubt greeted as heroes, they would have accomplished a great deal if all went well, much more than normally expected of such a small, unconventional band.

The main goal of the raid was no more ambitious than to deny the rebels use of the W&A line north of the Etowah River, simply by burning bridges, cutting rails on the single-track line, and disrupting telegraph communications. They would not try to disable locomotives or rolling stock encountered en route, attack or otherwise halt

APRIL 6, 1862

Andrews arrives at 3rd Division HQ to propose his plan to Gen. Mitchel

APRIL 7, 1862

Sunset: The raiders rendezvous with Andrews outside Shelbyville and set off

---

3 The only explosive available at the time was black powder. This was bulky and not very good for cutting iron rails. Dynamite was not patented until 1867.

4 A cord of wood is a stack 4 foot (122 cm) wide, 4 foot high, and 8 foot (244 cm) long—128 cubic feet (3.6 m³). The *General* averaged about 33 miles (53 km) per cord.

The Atlanta rail yard with more troops loaded on boxcars. The barely visible locomotive to the right-center is an American Standard 4-4-0 similar to the *General* and the *Texas*. To the right is the office of the *Daily Intelligencer* newspaper.

troop or supply trains, engage enemy forces, damage railroad facilities, or blow up the Tunnel Hill tunnel. If successful, Andrews' raiders would have performed an invaluable service by preventing rebels from sending trains north with troops, munitions, and supplies, and rendering them severely hampered in the withdrawal of troops, casualties, and materials. The area's road network was very poor, and the W&A was the only reliable means of moving large numbers of troops and supplies. It was hoped that stranded trains caught between Chattanooga and the burned bridges to the south would eventually be seized by Union forces, although realistically most would probably be destroyed by their operators.

There was apparently little thought of the long-term impact of the bridge-burnings. If Northern forces were able to immediately exploit the capture of Chattanooga and advance south toward Atlanta, even if they were able only to move part of the distance to gain a foothold in Georgia, the burned bridges would hamper their advance. If such an advance was delayed, the Confederates would no doubt quickly repair the bridges themselves, with the Yankees poised to advance from Chattanooga. Realistically Mitchel's lone division with limited logistics support would not be able to advance farther south without significant reinforcement, which would be slow in coming. When the Federals did resume the advance south there was little doubt that the Confederates would once again burn the bridges. Mitchel had a credible bridge-building capability but, nonetheless, burned bridges could delay an advance for weeks. As it was, these bridges would be burned and rebuilt numerous times before the war was over. The Etowah River Bridge itself was burned and rebuilt a total of six times.

The risks and costs for Mitchel were minimal. If the mission failed Mitchel was no worse off than he would have been if he had not ordered the attempt. The cost would be only a couple of dozen men and a small amount of money. Even if it failed overall it might create at least some degree of delay and confusion on the main Confederate rail line, although Mitchel undoubtedly envisaged himself accepting the surrender of the starved Chattanooga garrison within two weeks. At the time, Confederate forces in Chattanooga were weak and Mitchel hoped to reach the rail center before it could be reinforced. Andrews' raid might well help him achieve that goal.

From statements made by the men accompanying Andrews on the failed March raid attempt they were disconcerted and rattled by the experience. Andrews had asked the members of his first expedition and none were interested in a second chance of attaining glory. He learned that while he was comfortable operating behind Southern lines, that was not the case for conventional soldiers, who were entirely out of their element. Few, if any, had even been in the South in peacetime, much less performed as spies, an offense that led to the gallows. Andrews asked for volunteers who fully understood that they were embarking on a dangerous mission behind enemy lines. There was no time available for him to interview volunteers personally as he no doubt wished. He had his own preparations to make.

Mitchel took the simple expedient of having company commanders in one of his brigades recommend and select the men. They would know best who were steady, reliable, and resourceful. Andrews may also have specified men with strength, owing to the necessary heavy labor and their value in a close fight. He also requested some men who had been locomotive engineers or possessed other railroading experience.

Mitchel was born in Kentucky, but raised in Ohio and considered himself an Ohioan. He directed that the volunteers be selected from the 2nd, 20th, and 33rd Ohio Infantry Regiments of Col. Joshua W. Sill's 9th Brigade. Verbal orders were sent out before the meeting was concluded to the three regiments' company commanders, seeking men with soldierly qualities to volunteer for an unspecified secret mission. It is assumed that the company commanders chose the one or two men[5] from their units based on their knowledge of their abilities and character. Among them were one regimental sergeant major, two sergeants, seven corporals, and 12 privates. Very few knew one another. It is possible that Marion A. Ross, the 2nd Ohio's regimental sergeant major, was sent simply to have an overall military leader of the troops as he does not appear to have been detailed because of his martial knowledge and leadership ability. He had been in the Army for only a year, had been first promoted to regimental quartermaster sergeant and then sergeant major, the senior NCO in the regiment and basically an administrative assistant to the staff. He was considered somewhat of a dandy and attracted to military pomp and ceremony. At 29 he just did not fit the image of a hard-bitten experienced sergeant major. Not surprisingly Ross did not demonstrate any exceptional leadership talent or offer any military advice to Andrews.

On one level it seems unusual that an officer was not detailed so that the soldiers would be under formal military command rather than answering to a civilian. There are three reasons why this was not the case. Experienced officers were scarce; why risk one on a chancy secret mission? Also, why risk his reputation on the same? It just was not the kind of action for an officer and gentleman to be involved with. It could be, too, that it was simply to prevent any leadership and authority conflicts between Andrews and an officer, especially one inexperienced in such sordid affairs. Andrews had formulated the plan, he knew the rail line and its operation intimately, and was in the best position to make immediate decisions with regards to rapidly changing circumstances, even if he lacked military experience.

For the most part the volunteer raiders had little combat experience. Most of these men had volunteered between August and November 1861, with a few having

Photographs are available of all of the Andrews raiders, but most were taken after, often long after, their April 1862 exploits. This photograph of Pvt. John R. Porter of Company G, 21st Ohio is one of the few available photographs taken before the raid. Porter missed the train, but was later identified as a member of the Andrews party, imprisoned with the other raiders, but successfully escaped. He was the last of the raiders to pass away, in 1923. (Bogle)

---

5 21st Ohio sent two men each from its Companies C, F, and G.

APRIL 11, 1862

Gen. Mitchel seizes Huntsville

Andrews' raiders	Parent unit	Birth–Death
James J. Andrews†	Civilian of Kentucky	1829–1862
Pvt. William Bensinger‡	Co. G, 21st Ohio	1840–1918
Pvt. Wilson W. Brown*	Co. F, 21st Ohio	1837–1916
Pvt. Robert Buffum‡	Co. H, 21st Ohio	1828–1871
William H. Campbell†	Civilian of Ohio	1839–1862
Cpl. Daniel A. Dorsey*	Co. H, 33rd Ohio	1838-1918
Pvt. William J. Knight*	Co. E, 21st Ohio	1837-1916
Sgt. Elihu H. Mason‡	Co. K, 21st Ohio	1831–1896
Cpl. Jacob Parrott‡	Co. K, 33rd Ohio	1843–1908
Cpl. William C. Pittenger‡	Co. G, 2nd Ohio	1840–1904
Cpl. William H.H. Reddick‡	Co. B, 33rd Ohio	1840–1903
Pvt. Samuel Robertson†	Co. G, 33rd Ohio	1842–1862
Sgt. Maj. Marion A. Ross†	Staff, 2nd Ohio	1832–1862
Sgt. John M. Scott†	Co. F, 21st Ohio	1839–1862
Pvt. Charles P. Shadrach†	Co. K, 2nd Ohio	1840–1862
Pvt. Samuel Slavens†	Co. E, 33rd Ohio	1831–1862
Pvt. George D. Wilson†	Co. B, 2nd Ohio	1830–1862
Pvt. John Alfred Wilson*	Co. C, 21st Ohio	1832–1904
Pvt. John Wollam*	Co. C, 33rd Ohio	1840–1890
Cpl. Mark Wood*	Co. C, 21st Ohio	1839–1866
Raiders who did not participate in the chase:		
Cpl. Martin J. Hawkins*	Co. A, 22nd Ohio	1830–1886
Cpl. Samuel Llewellyn§	Co. I, 33rd Ohio	1841–1915
Pvt. John R. Porter*	Co. G, 21st Ohio	1838–1923
Pvt. James O.W. Smith§	Co. I, 2nd Ohio	1844–1868

Escaped †Executed ‡Exchanged
§ Impressed into Confederate service and deserted.
Name Notes: Pvt Shadrach's real name was Philip G., which he disliked, and usually listed his name as Charles P. or Perry D. His last name is sometimes incorrectly spelled "Sharack."
Pvt Wollam is sometimes incorrectly listed as "Whollan," "Wollen," or "Wollum."
William Campbell is often erroneously listed as a "citizen of Kentucky" and informed his captors he was in Company K, 2nd Ohio.

enrolled earlier in the year in the 2nd Ohio on three-month enlistments and when soon discharged reenlisted for a further three years. They were dedicated to the cause, but most had seen no action in their short time in the Army. Some had fought in the Battle of Ivy Mountain, Kentucky,[6] on November 8–9, 1861, a minor action against Confederate cavalry raiders. Most were between 17 and 25 years of age. The youngest was 16, Pvt. Smith, and the oldest were Pvt. George Wilson and Cpl. Hawkins, both 32. Most of the men were farmers or tradesmen with between

---

6 Not to be confused with the 1864 Battle of Ivy Point Hill, Kentucky.

THE RAIDERS' REVOLVERS

There is seldom any mention of the makes and models used by the raiders. Being from infantry units, to which revolvers were not issued, it can only be surmised that they obtained non-issue side arms. Officers bought their own revolvers, and it was not uncommon for rankers to unofficially do the same. The raiders' handguns would have been obtained either from officers or friends, as none were available to purchase locally. A revolver of the period was expensive and a private made $13 a month; Government cost for a Colt was $25. The most common makes were Adams, Colt, Kerr, Lefaucheux, LeMat, Remington, Savage, Starr, and Whitney. The Colt was very popular, and expensive, with the two most common models being the .44-cal Model 1860 Army and .36-cal Model 1851 Navy. "Navy" models were used almost as widely by soldiers as "Army" models. The one confirmed revolver carried by a raider was indeed a Colt Navy Model 1851. Andrews himself carried a pearl-handled Colt. Other widely used handguns were the Remington New Model 1861 Army .44-cal and Navy .36-cal models, plus the Star .44-cal Army Model. Some may have had only small-caliber pocket pistols. There was little standardization of calibers and cartridges, with most makes having their own unique ammunition. No doubt several types of ammunition were carried by the raiders. These were all single-action, percussion six-shooters. These revolvers used conical bullets held, glued, in a combustible paper or linen cartridge containing the black powder charge. Cartridges were packed in six-round packets and the raiders may have carried about six packets. One account describes "a liberal supply of cartridges."

To load these weapons was a time-consuming process. The hammer was placed at half-cock and a cartridge was inserted into the chamber from the cylinder's front and the bullet pressed in with the thumb. The cylinder was rotated by hand to align the loaded chamber over the trigger. The loading lever under the barrel was pulled downward to ram the bullet solidly into the chamber and compress the powder ensuring positive combustion. This process was continued until all chambers were loaded. Next a percussion cap was pressed by the thumb on to the cone (or nipple) over each chamber on the rear end of the cylinder. The cylinder was again rotated by hand until all nipples were capped. The piece was taken off half-cock and it was ready for action. Sometimes non-combustible paper cartridges were used and the lower end had to be torn open with the teeth, the powder poured into the chamber, and the remaining paper worn off and spat out before inserting the bullet. Certainly loading a revolver was not something one could easily do on the run or at a mounted trot.

six and eight months' military experience. Nearsighted Cpl. Pittenger was a schoolteacher and Cpl. Llewellyn a coal miner. Pvt. Robertson was a sawmill engineer, prep-school-educated Sergeant Major Ross was an accomplished musician, and Cpl. Jacob Parrott was an illiterate farmer.

In some companies, word of the need for volunteers to undertake a secret expedition was spread by mouth. In others the captain called together a small group of men thought capable, and one man was selected. In still others the commander went directly to an individual or two he thought suited for such an undertaking. Those selected and consenting were ordered to report to their regimental commander. They were given no details of what the mission would entail other than they would be embarking on a dangerous operation behind Southern lines under the command of a civilian.

Besides manpower Andrews needed experienced locomotive engineers who would drive the stolen train, serve as a fireman, and teach the other men how to operate as a brakeman[7] and other duties. He also needed backups or alternates for these assignments. This was fortuitous as two of his experienced railroaders failed to make it to the train the morning it departed Marietta. All the men were interviewed by Andrews himself to determine the extent of their skills, knowledge, and experience.

Privates Knight and Brown had both been locomotive engineers, the first in Indiana and Illinois and the second with the Mobile & Ohio RR. Pvt. Smith had been a machinist for the Columbus & Indiana Central RR and Cpl. Hawkins, the most experienced engineer, a locomotive engineer in Pennsylvania. However, Smith and Hawkins missed boarding the train at Marietta. Cpl. Wood was also a machinist and strangely an Englishman.

The only other civilian besides Andrews was William Campbell, an experienced locomotive engineer. Campbell appears to have been a shady individual. The reason for his unofficial presence in the camp of the 2nd Ohio is unknown, although it may have had something to do with his reported reputation. It has been suggested that he was visiting friends there as a means of avoiding inquiries from the law; there were stories that he may have murdered a man. Described as a hulking, bullying type, it appears he volunteered for adventure and perhaps some degree of profit. Being a civilian, and considering his background, there can be little doubt that Andrews paid him for his services.

Mitchel provided Andrews with an unknown sum of money for the purchase of civilian clothing, food, and other items. The raiders also needed money en route for meals, hotels, and train tickets. This he disbursed to the men on the night of the 7th. It is not known how much Andrews was paid for his services. Rumors have it anywhere from $20,000 to $50,000 in gold. This was a considerable sum in 1862, $20,000 being equivalent to $425,000 today. But is doubtful if his fee was that high. Another story is that he was paid an unspecified but not inconsiderable sum, plus the right to trade freely across the lines for up to $5,000 in transactions per month.

The infantry volunteers would, of course, receive no financial reward. No doubt there were some glory seekers among them, but they were motivated mainly by a strong sense of duty. They had not seen any real war, having been occupied with training, encampments, and marching into Alabama. They had wintered in Ohio, near home, and their present situation found them camped in the South in spring weather and with no enemy in sight. Many wanted to see some action, being young, enthusiastic, and naive to the horrors of war.

In the morning the men were given money and a pass to nearby Shelbyville, with a population of a few hundred. They were instructed to purchase appropriate civilian clothes and food, and, even though this is seldom mentioned in accounts, to purchase or borrow pistols. There were none available in such a small town, especially one that had been under Southern control and now had an occupying army present. There were only a few dry goods and general stores, and their inventories were no doubt

---

7 Locomotives had no brakes. To stop, the engine was reversed and brake wheels set on the tender and cars.

sparse. One man, Cpl Dorsey, was unable to find fitting civilian pants and began the adventure wearing dark blue issue trousers. Others borrowed civilian clothing from friends, perhaps because there was insufficient available in town or perhaps just to hang on to the money given them. What little clothing was available was cotton rather than the preferred wool: caps, coats, vests, checkered shirts, trousers or denim jeans, mostly in brown or butternut (yellowish light brown).

As they rummaged through camp and prepared for their departure, rumors spread like wildfire. It was no secret within the 9th Brigade that something was afoot, but the exact nature of this secret expedition remained unknown. Among the bored soldiers in an idle encampment this must have been exciting news as it could easily have heralded impending action for the rest.

Some men were lightheartedly advised they were marching to their doom, never to be seen again. Other raiders bid their comrades a fond farewell and received their best wishes. Most penned quick letters to loved ones and made arrangements to secure their arms and personal effects within their companies.

At sunset on the 7th, the Monday, the men assembled at their regimental headquarters and were picked up by ambulances dispatched by division or simply went on their own to the rendezvous specified by Andrews, a knoll covered with dead trees just off the Shelbyville–Wartrace Road about a mile (1.6 km) east of Shelbyville. They were to meet Andrews clandestinely that night for instructions. They all traveled by foot to the rendezvous carrying their kit and merged into a conspicuous group by the time they arrived.

The raiders were prepared to depart that night. The sky was clouding over, but the young moon was visible as lightning heralded the approach of a coming rainstorm. It was an odd group of individuals, which hardly could be termed a "unit," that was expected to infiltrate cross-country into enemy territory, covertly travel among the enemy, steal a train deep within the Confederacy in broad daylight, and rush north wreaking havoc and destruction. They had no special training or experience in such affairs, had never worked together before, and were completely unaware of what they were getting into. They were simply a gang of adventurous riflemen trained in repetitious drill, marching in mass formations, and doing everything uniformly as a cohesive body. Most were ill-prepared for duplicity, and uncomfortable with violating the formal conventions of warfare as was now expected of them. They knew their leader only by reputation and what they did know was probably only through inflated campfire rumors.

Andrews first briefly described the mission and its aim in a quiet voice to the attentive soldiers. He told them bluntly, as later recalled by Cpl. Pittenger, "Soldiers, if you are detected while engaged in this business, the great possibility is that you will be put to death—hung [sic] as spies, or massacred by a mob." He was no doubt familiar with the fate of the November bridge burners. Andrews told them that if they were unwilling to take the risks, they were to return to camp and say nothing of this meeting to anyone. All present declared they would follow him, no doubt feeling that the promise of adventure was more attractive than the endless boring picket duty and fatigues with their regiments.

Andrews provided each member of the raiding party with specific instructions on how they were to make their way to Chattanooga to catch a W&A train to Marietta. They could also catch a train on the Memphis & Charleston RR west of Chattanooga for a ride to that city and then transfer to the W&A. They would first travel east through Wartrace and Manchester, Tennessee. In this way it would not seem as though they had traveled through Union forces on their way south. Andrews explained how they were to pass themselves off as Kentuckians from Fleming County

A clandestine meeting on the Shelbyville-Wartrace Road about a mile (1.6 km) east of Shelbyville, Tennessee on the night of April 7, 1862. It was here, on a low hillock during an approaching thunderstorm, that the raiders met for the first time and a bearded James Andrews gave them the details of their mission. (Pittenger)

in the northeast corner of the state and declared there were no Kentuckians from that county in Confederate service who could trip them up. It is uncertain how he could be so confident of this fact, even if he had previously resided in Flemingsburg.

When one of the volunteers asked what they were to do if they were suspected under questioning and could not get away or talk themselves out of their situation, "Enlist without hesitation in the rebel army," Andrews advised the surprised soldiers. They would not be considered deserters and, sooner or later, perhaps while on picket some dark night, they could make good their escape and return to their regiment and friends. "The difficulty is to keep out of the Southern army, not to get into it."

Andrews discussed in minimal detail their actions upon stealing the train in Marietta. They would run it as close as they could toward advancing Union forces, hopefully through Chattanooga and, turning west, straight to Mitchel's division. If they could not get that far they would abandon the train and make their way through Confederate lines as a body.

They were to break up in teams of two to four men for the cross-country trip to Chattanooga. Andrews himself would travel by horse and provide any assistance necessary to the squads he encountered. They had to be at the specified rendezvous in Marietta by Thursday evening, the 10th. They had just three days to make their way there; the last train departing Chattanooga for Marietta on the 10th was at 5:00 PM and they all had to be aboard it. On Friday morning of the 11th they would catch the northbound train.

Forming six or seven squads Andrews moved from group to group disbursing the Confederate money and answering questions. They were now committed, and he gave them the details of the plan, to include the movements of the 3rd Division, whose advance they were supporting.

Mitchel would march on Huntsville that coming morning and planned to capture the city by Friday, the day the raiders would steal their train. Mitchel would then turn east toward Chattanooga. The raiders, speeding north aboard their stolen locomotive, would burn the bridges that same day to block reinforcements. He told them they would also be encountering southbound trains that they would have to deal with.

As a torrent of rain fell amid lightning flashes, Andrews firmly shook each man's hand and gave his good wishes. They started eastward down the muddy road. It would rain for the next ten days. No one yet appreciated the impact the ceaseless rains would have on the Chattanooga Railroad Expedition.

APRIL 12, 1862

3:00–4:00 AM
Andrews briefs raiders in the Marietta Hotel

THE RAID

Cross-country into Dixie

That first wet night on the road did nothing to improve the expectations of the raiders as they trudged down a muddy road toward Wartrace, the last Union outpost. They hoped to get beyond their own picket lines, which could be as dangerous as rebel pickets on such a night. They soon became discouraged by the rain, mud, and cold, and sought shelter, but there was little to be found in the sparsely populated country. Some found barns; others demanded accommodation in homes after rousing slumbering inhabitants. They found Wartrace occupied by Union cavalrymen disinclined to let them pass, but Andrews successfully cleared the way as he was to do so often in the coming days.

With so few roads, it was inevitable that two or three squads would join up. Some were able to catch rides on wagons driven by locals. Meals of the "coarsest fare" were purchased en route. There were indiscretions on the road south—one man became drunk and talkative and had to be kept quiet by two comrades until he sobered up; others overdramatized their roles as pro-secessionists to the point of being unbelievable to locals. One squad made such extravagant claims and provided contradictory answers to questions that a group of rebel guerrillas was sent to pursue the suspicious strangers, but they managed to elude the searchers, who eventually called off their hunt. Two men, however, fared worse.

Cpl. Llewellyn and Pvt. Ovid Smith traveling together had aroused suspicions and were arrested by militiamen in Jasper. Their story about seeking a Kentucky regiment persuaded no one, and the fact that they were traveling without baggage raised suspicions. They were turned over to the nearest Confederate post and "persuaded" to enlist. They soon found themselves in an artillery unit defending Chattanooga of all places. At the end of April their new unit engaged their own 3rd Division and Llewellyn fled across a bridge in the midst of battle. This called attention to Smith and he was accused and court-martialed for disloyalty. He eventually ended up in the Chattanooga Jail with the raiders, but he was never connected with them. He served his sentence, was released to his unit in September, and soon managed to desert and return to the 2nd Ohio.

As the squads trekked through the beautiful Cumberland Mountains, some encountered furloughed rebel soldiers and engaged them in conversation to learn local news. Most of the groups wisely designated a man or two as spokespersons who could tell a good story about their reason for passing through. Reportedly, some of the Midwesterners were so bold as to affect passable Southern accents. Even with the suspicious nature of the border inhabitants, the raiders found the locals to be easily deceived in most cases. All forms of travelers were found on the road: men journeying to join one side or the other, smugglers, drifters, deserters, merchants, slave-hunters, and assorted riffraff. Some were challenged by militiamen suggesting they join their unit rather than seeking out a Kentuckian regiment. In Manchester, Cpl. Dorsey was finally able to exchange his Union blue trousers for "less conspicuous" yellow-and-white striped pants.

They pressed on through the intermittent rains seeking room and board where they could. Their average of 30 miles (64 km) a day was good on such undeveloped roads, but insufficient for them to meet their deadline. Some squads were planning on walking through Wednesday night as they were still as much as 40 miles (48 km) from Chattanooga. Pittenger's squad learned from another they joined that Andrews was passing word that the mission was postponed by one day because of the slow progress due to the rain.

APRIL 12, 1862

5:00 AM
The raiders board the *General*, bound for Big Shanty

APRIL 12, 1862

6:00 AM
The raiders steal the *General*

This was welcome news to the wet, tired travelers, but it was to prove a major setback for the expedition's successes. Andrews unilaterally made the decision based on his knowledge of the difficulties in moving large bodies of troops in such conditions. However, he failed to consider the energy and determination of the fiery little general. Mitchel did not delay his advance for a day, but drove his miserable troops onward through the downpour and high creeks. Rather than meeting in Marietta on Thursday night, the 10th, they could arrive Friday. To Andrews, unused to the military's slavishness to time schedules, a day's delay would cause no harm. He habitually adjusted his own schedule because of the nature of his work; this was his first major mistake.

Some of the squads reached the swollen Tennessee River near Jasper on Wednesday night and made arrangements to be ferried across. Rebel cavalrymen questioned the strangers but, unlike Llewellyn and Smith's, their stories were accepted. Dorsey reported, "We made it a point to appear as insignificant and uneducated as possible."

That night, news of the battle at Shiloh spread with claims it was a great Yankee defeat. This did little to hearten the raiders. More bad news arrived the following morning: a messenger arrived with orders that no one was allowed across the Tennessee River for the next three days. Word was that Mitchel was advancing on Huntsville and that there might be Yankee spies about. With this discouraging news, and unable to convince the ferry operator that they could help the Southern cause by being allowed to continue south to join their unit, they continued east on foot, despite many of the party now suffering from head colds.

Most of the squads were stacking up on the north side of the river, and the rugged mountain terrain drastically wasted away the grace time. In fact over half of the raiders had now joined up and were urgently looking for a means to cross the river. They were able to talk a ferryman into taking them across in a storm and were delighted to find the weather had precluded the setting of a guard at the far landing. One squad managed to catch a ride on the westbound train to Chattanooga loaded with Shiloh wounded. While a few had managed to catch an earlier train, most barely reached Chattanooga in time for that day's last departure to Marietta. It was Friday the 11th. Mitchel had seized Huntsville that morning.

There was standing room only and the cars were filled with Confederate soldiers and boastful, mostly drunken civilians confident the Yankees would be defeated. Some of the raiders were concerned about the expedition's success, no doubt anxious in the presence of this many Southern travelers. Others were more positive, even with the many delays and the changes to their plans. Finally they were approaching their goal and were buoyed by the irrepressible enthusiasm of their leader.

It soon became apparent that the poor condition of the wartime rail line and running at night forced the train to run very slowly—with a maximum speed of 18 mph (29 km per hour) they had a seven-hour ride ahead of them. This concerned some of the raiders, who thought high speed was essential for their mission and survival. Although they were traveling the same route that they would cover the next day, it was impossible to study the land at night. They stopped for supper at Dalton and, passing Camp McDonald, they would have been able to see the many campfires. At midnight the slumbering raiders were roused with the announcement, "Marietta!"

All but two of the raiders took rooms in the Fletcher House (later Kennesaw House), a hotel adjacent to the railroad station, with several men bedding in the second-floor rooms. Cpl. Martin Hawkins and Pvt. John Porter had arrived earlier and took a room in the Marietta Hotel. They failed to tip the clerk. Consequently, he failed to wake them in the pre-dawn hours to catch the departing train. Hawkins was the most experienced engineer, but his duties would have to be assumed by Pvt. Wilson Brown. It is possible that Andrews received information from a contact here, Henry G. Cole, owner of the Marietta Hotel and a known Unionist, but this is unconfirmed.

Andrews woke the men after only a few hours' sleep and informed them all of their individual duties. They dressed in the dark and about half were summoned to Andrews' room where he laid out more details. It was here that Sgt. Maj. Ross was so bold as to propose the enterprise be abandoned. He reasoned that the enemy's vigilance was heightened owing to Mitchel's advance; guards would be increased at stations, and the line blocked by unscheduled southbound trains. On their way south they had witnessed for themselves the huge rebel presence at Big Shanty. Andrews quietly reasoned with each fear: that their mission was to support Mitchel's advance, that there were sidings to bypass oncoming trains, that their story that they were on a special assignment to head north was plausible, and that the rebels at Big Shanty would provide a false sense of security and the train would indeed be left unattended. His arguments were not entirely convincing and others joined Ross, although their protests were perhaps not as vigorous. Andrews refused to consider abandoning another operation and returning in disgrace. He argued that what they were about to do would be completely unexpected. Dramatically he closed with, "I will accomplish my purpose or leave my bones to bleach in Dixie." Andrews added that if any man wished to quit, he could take a train in the opposite direction and work his way back to Union lines. With that seeming to be just as dangerous as stealing a train they agreed to obey his orders, and started out for the station.

Pvt. "Alf" Wilson later wrote the following about how they regarded their prospects at the start of the operation: "Our doom might be fixed before the setting of another sun. We might be hanging to the limbs of some trees along the railroad, with an enraged populace jeering and shouting vengeance because we had no more lives to give up; or we might leave a trail of fire and destruction behind us, and come triumphantly rolling into Chattanooga and Huntsville...to receive the welcome plaudits of comrades left behind, and the thanks of our general, and the praises of a grateful people."

The train-stealers

Andrews collected his raiders together, no doubt flustered by the absence of four men, one being the much-needed engineer, Hawkins. There was no time to run back to the Marietta Hotel to check on the two men there. With no known reason for their disappearance he was forced to hide his concerns that the mission might be compromised. He reportedly gave his final instructions:

> Get seats near each other in the same car and of course say nothing of our business on the way up. When the train makes the Big Shanty breakfast stop, keep your places till I tell you to go. If anything unexpected happens, look to me for the lead. Knight, Brown, and Alfred Wilson will go with me to the engine. The rest will go on the left of the train forward of where we'll uncouple it. [Camp McDonald was on the opposite side.] Climb into the cars as quickly as you can when the order is given. If anyone interferes, shoot him, but don't fire unless you have to.

They purchased tickets to different destinations and scattered out on the platform just as the first morning Atlanta–Chattanooga passenger/freight chugged in at 5:00 AM having departed Atlanta one hour previously. It was scheduled to arrive at

THE CHASE BEGINS: 5:00 AM TO 10:00 AM
APRIL 12, 1862

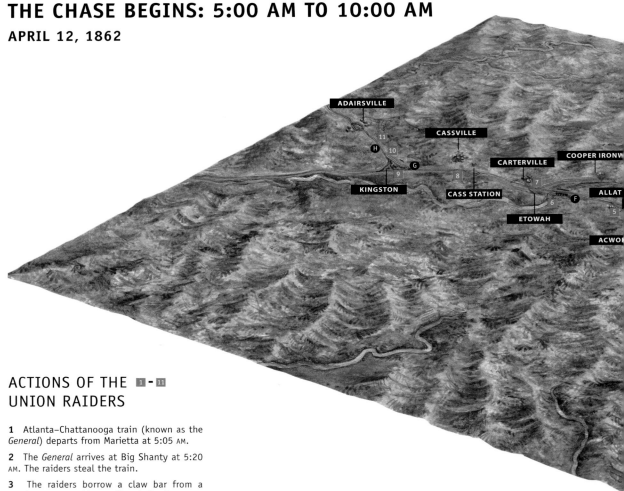

ACTIONS OF THE 1 - 11
UNION RAIDERS

1 Atlanta–Chattanooga train (known as the *General*) departs from Marietta at 5:05 AM.

2 The *General* arrives at Big Shanty at 5:20 AM. The raiders steal the train.

3 The raiders borrow a claw bar from a section gang working at Moon's Station.

4 The raiders cut the telegraph wire and erect a barricade.

5 The raiders dismount from the *General*, lift a rail, and cut the telegraph wire outside of Allatoona.

6 The *General* crosses the Etowa River at 8:00 AM and spots the *Yonah* locomotive on the Etowah railroad.

7 The raiders cut the telegraph wire outside of Carterville and erect two barricades.

8 The raiders collect wood and water for the *General* at Cass Station.

9 The *General* is delayed for over one hour at Kingston by three southbound trains. It eventually departs at 9:35 AM.

10 The raiders erect a barricade and cut the telegraph wire just north of Kingston.

11 A rail is lifted further outside of Kingston.

ACTIONS OF THE A - H
CONFEDERATE PURSUERS

A The Atlanta–Chattanooga train departs from Atlanta at 4:00 AM.

B Fuller and Murphy pursue the *General* on foot. Kendrick is dispatched to Marietta to telegraph Atlanta with the news.

C Fuller and Murphy reach Moon's Station and continue the pursuit on a handcar.

D The pursuers arm themselves in Acworth.

E The pursuers' handcar is derailed outside Allatoona. They continue the pursuit on foot again.

F The pursuers commandeer the *Yonah* locomotive at Etowah and continue the pursuit.

G Fuller commandeers the *William R. Smith* locomotive at Kingston.

H The *William R. Smith* is halted outside of Kingston by a lifted rail. Fuller and Murphy continue to Adairsville on foot. The engineer for the *William R. Smith* replaces the rail and continues.

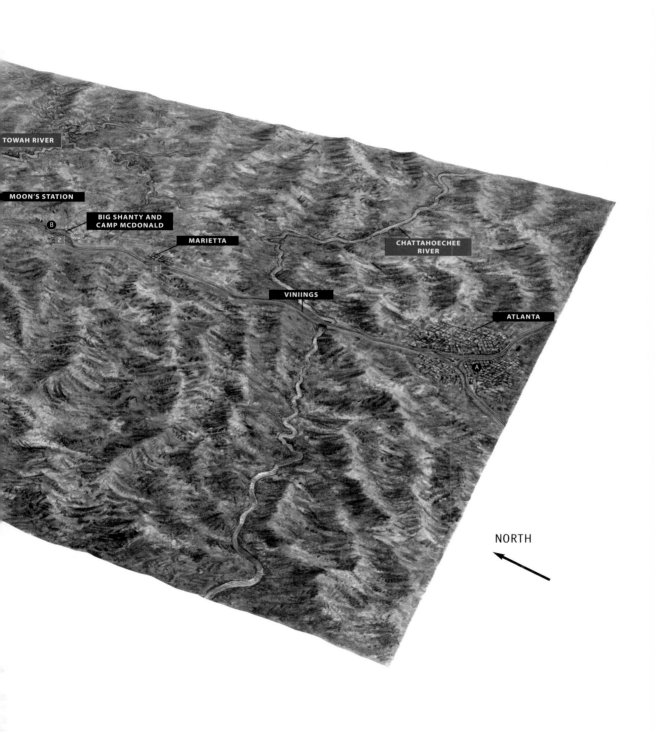

TOWAH RIVER

MOON'S STATION

BIG SHANTY AND
CAMP MCDONALD

MARIETTA

CHATTAHOECHEE
RIVER

VINIINGS

ATLANTA

NORTH

Chattanooga at 3:40 PM and the soldiers were provided with vouchers for the $5 fare. The two passenger cars, partly filled with passengers from Atlanta, were filling up fast. Ahead of them were a mail and baggage car and three empty boxcars, the ideal arrangement for their plan. A tall stern-looking conductor wearing a deep blue coat and checkered trousers stepped off the train and shouted, "All aboard!" The raiders boarded through different cars, but all ended up in the front, with most having to stand. With a jerk the train started off on the 8-mile (13 km) run to Big Shanty, curving around Kennesaw Mountain, the site of a future vicious battle. The apprehension of the raiders can well be imagined. The late sleepers, Hawkins and Porter, did rush to the station but were in time only to watch the train disappear into the distance. They must have realized with sinking hearts that not only had they failed to succeed in their military mission but that they were also abandoned in hostile territory. Taking a later train would only find them trapped by burning bridges—or so they assumed. Instead, they decided to venture into the countryside to avoid people.

With a shout of "Big Shanty!" and "Twenty minutes for breakfast," the conductor would have announced the train's arrival. The locomotive, known as the *General*, rolled to a halt in front of the two-story Lacy Hotel, opposite a vast field of white tents. Guards paced along the camp's perimeter only 50 feet (15 m) from the puffing locomotive.

Camp McDonald was occupied by some 7,000 recruits, mustered the month before, of the 39th–43rd and 52nd Infantry Regiments, Georgia Volunteers as well as the 9th Georgia Infantry Battalion. They were mostly unarmed at this point. The 42nd, by coincidence, was scheduled to depart by rail for Mississippi the following day. It was no doubt disconcerting to the raiders to peer out the windows and see fields covered by tightly packed tents and patrolling guards, even if they only shouldered pikes.

There were fears that part of the crew would remain aboard and that force would have to be applied. But in fact all the crew and most of the passengers hurried off the train and into the hotel. The raiders stayed seated. Pittenger described it as, "... a

The final briefing on the night of April 11 in a second-floor Fletcher House guest room where James Andrews detailed each man's duties. The men caught only a few hours of sleep with three or four to a room. (Pittenger)

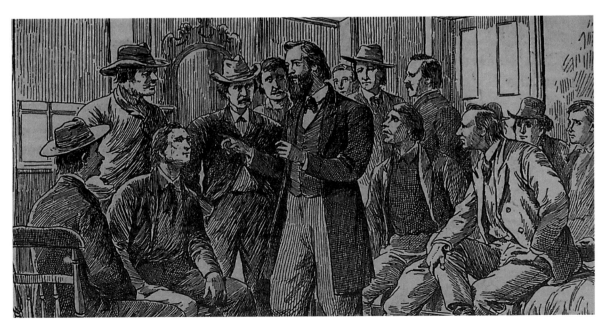

thrilling moment! Victory or death hung on the next minute!" Others must have felt ice water in their veins. Andrews, elegantly dressed with a top hat and carrying his saddlebags, nonchalantly walked forward to ensure there was no train ahead on the main line, calmly stepped into the car and gave the word to go.

Unloading, they wandered forward toward the boxcars. Accounts differ on which side of the train they approached the boxcar, whether the camp or hotel side. They were indifferent to attracting attention now—in just a few moments they would once again be soldiers facing the enemy.

Everyone moved into position. The passenger cars were quietly uncoupled by engineer William Knight. Then he, assistant engineer Wilson Brown, and fireman Alfred Wilson climbed into the *General*. "Alf" Wilson climbed on to a boxcar and spun the brake wheel. Andrews signaled the other 16 men into the last boxcar and stepped into the *General*'s cab after throwing the switch on to the main line. Knight cut the conductor's bell rope, checked the steam pressure, released the tender's brakes, and opened the steam lever. The men in the boxcar shut the door as defense against musket balls and suddenly felt cut off and blind. Every jerk and jolt of starting up sent alarm through them. It was 110 rail miles (177 km) to Chattanooga.

As the raiders picked up speed on the rough rails, no doubt their heart rates quickened too. In a matter of hours they hoped to reach their destination covered in glory. The men in the boxcar's gloom were startled when they suddenly rumbled to a stop. Sliding open the door they were told that the boiler needed stoking; the steam was down. The men were fearful that the delay meant pursuers could catch up with them, but it took only a few minutes to raise the steam pressure. Andrews was unconcerned with pursuit by another train. Atlanta was over 30 miles (48 km) behind them and Kingston, the next place locomotives could be found, was almost 30 miles (48 km) ahead. It was about 6:00 AM.

Before the locomotive thieves could take off at full speed they would have to keep to the scheduled run time of only 16 mph (26 km per hour). Only one scheduled southbound train was expected in the morning and it was supposed to be on a siding in Kingston when they arrived. However, if this train had proceeded south, there were sidings en route for one train or the other to switch on to. After Kingston they expected to meet a regular freight train and then a passenger one.

They slowed down at Moon's Station where a section gang under Jackson Bond was working on a siding. Bond was concerned with the early arrival, lack of passenger cars, and the strange faces in the cab. They stopped long enough for Wilson Brown to talk a railhand out of a claw bar to use to pry up rail tracks.

They soon halted again to check the engine and cut the telegraph wire, and it was John Scott's job to scramble up the 20 foot (6 m) pole and drag the wire down. A hacksaw found in the *General* was used to cut it twice and they took the yards of wire with them to prevent it being spliced back in.[8] At the same time they stacked crossties on the track and others pulled down a telegraph pole, adding it to the barricade. Andrews was ecstatic with the progress thus far and exuded confidence. Fortunately, their early departure from Big Shanty put them ahead of schedule.

At Acworth they quickly inspected and oiled the engine, leaving waiting passengers confused on the platform. Speeding through Allatoona, they laughed at startled waiting passengers. However, at that station they spotted a small unidentified yard engine on a siding. To halt its possible use to pursue them they halted outside of Allatoona to cut the wire and pry up a rail. This proved extremely difficult. With

8 Telegraph wire was uninsulated galvanized 6-gauge (0.1620 in/4.115 mm).

THE *GENERAL*

The *General*, the locomotive stolen by Andrews' raiders, was a design known as the American Standard or "eight-wheeler." It is not known what "general" she was named after. The 50,000 pound (22,680 kg) locomotive was built to order for the W&ARR in 1855 by the Rogers, Ketchum and Grosvenor Locomotive Works in Paterson, New Jersey for $8,850. She was what is known under the Whyte classification as a 4-4-0, that is, four small forward-leading pilot or pony wheels (two pairs of axles with four wheels), four much larger drive wheels 60 inches (152 cm) in diameter, and no rear trailing wheels (beneath the cab). The eight-wheel tender had a capacity of 1.75 cords of wood (just under what can be carried in two modern full-size pickup trucks) and 1,750 gallons (6,624 liters) of water. The *General* could reach a speed of 60 mph (97 km per hour) and was known on the line as a fast runner. When recovered at the end of the great chase it was found the *General* had suffered no damage other than a brass journal bearing needing replacement. She was back in service two weeks later. Ironically it was the *General* that carried the captured raiders from Chattanooga to Atlanta. In September 1864, with Federal forces closing in on Atlanta, the *General* and four other locomotives and their freight cars were burned and the *General* was rammed into another locomotive. She was briefly taken over by the U.S. Military Railroad Service but not repaired, and was returned to the W&A in 1866. In the 1870s and 1880s the *General* underwent rebuilding and upgrading, including being converted to coal burning.

In 1888 the *General* traveled to Columbus, Ohio, to attend the National Encampment of the Grand Army of the Republic. The Nashville, Chattanooga & St. Louis RR leased the W&A line in 1890 and received the *General*. In 1892 she was finally retired from regular service, but still towed to other cities for commemorative display. She was put on display in the Union Depot at Chattanooga in 1893, and this led to an ownership dispute. Up to the 1950s the *General* was frequently displayed about the country in expositions and fairs.

In great secrecy the *General* was moved to Nashville, Tennessee for restoration in 1961 and converted to run on fuel oil. Again operational in 1962 she undertook an extensive series of tours until 1966, the last time she ran under her own steam. In 1967 the *General* was to be returned to the state of Georgia, but it was halted in Chattanooga and kept there. This resulted in a legal battle, with the U.S. Supreme Court ruling in 1970 that the historic locomotive be returned to Georgia. In 1972 she was moved to the Big Shanty Museum in Kennesaw. The *General* remains there in what is now the Southern Museum of Civil War and Locomotive History.

only a claw bar and crossties as poor levers they worked at lifting a rail and, while ultimately successful, it was far too time-consuming. They needed more claw or lining bars, tamping picks, and spike mauls. The rail they lifted into a boxcar so it could not be reinstalled, and engineer Knight craftily fixed a red handkerchief on a staff to the cowcatcher. This warned that an "extra" train followed or there was danger on the line behind the train. This would delay sending southbound trains through after the raiders passed.

At 8:00 AM the *General* passed over the 620 foot-long (189 m) Etowah River Bridge (320 foot-wide [98 m] river) on its five massive stone pillars. No effort was made to set it on fire. It was not a covered bridge and it was still raining lightly. On the far side was Etowah junction and at the spur switch sat a steamed-up locomotive belonging to the Etowah Manufacturing and Mining Company. The 2.5-mile (4 km) spur led to the Cooper Iron Works, an important source of iron for the South. This old engine was the *Yonah*. Andrews did not expect it to be there and was unaware even of its existence, despite the many runs he had made on the line. The *Yonah* was potentially a serious threat and the crew watched the *General* clickety-clack past with open curiosity. Railroad men are acutely aware of disrupted schedules and unusual patterns. Engineer Knight suggested to Andrews that "We had better destroy that engine and the bridge with it."

The 620-foot-long (189 m) Etowah River Bridge in 1864. Andrews failed to burn this trestle bridge, considered a grave error by many. The entrenchments in the foreground were dug by Union troops during the Atlanta Campaign. Today this area is heavily forested and the bridge is gone, but the stone pillars remain. (National Archives)

Andrews may have considered that Big Shanty was 17 miles (27 km) behind them and with the rail and telegraph cut there was no chance of word getting to Etowah or beyond. He may also have been attempting to avoid any confrontation that might lead to shooting, as his experience as a spy discouraged overt action. They had bluffed or simply sped their way through to this point, and he probably wished to continue the charade as long as possible. He also planned to cut the rail and wire up ahead and then, of course, there would be bridge burnings. Andrews appears to have been confident that the hardest part of the mission, simply stealing the train, had been accomplished. "It won't make any difference," Andrews commented to the other members of the raiding party.

They were on schedule or a little ahead, and naively comfortable that there was as yet no pursuit.

"Someone is running off with your train!"

Further down the line it was a different matter though. Having washed up and sitting down to a 25-cent breakfast, Fuller and his crew needed to rush through the meal to stay on schedule. Besides Conductor Fuller, the *General* was crewed by E. Jefferson "Jeff" Cain, fireman Andrew "Andy" Anderson, and the A&W foreman of machinery and motive power, Anthony Murphy. The latter was on his way to inspect new machinery at Allatoona. A loud huffing noise startled them and Murphy reportedly shouted to Fuller, "Someone is running off with your train!"[9]

A great deal of turmoil arose and people ran to the windows. Bounding outside, Fuller asked a guard who had taken the train. His answer led Fuller to believe it may have been deserters from the camp. Fuller later stated that he had noticed a larger number of passengers than usual at Marietta and that a disproportionate number were young men. He recognized Andrews by sight, his being a frequent

---

9 The accounts of Fuller and Murphy in regard to the chase are often in conflict and they disagreed on many aspects to the end of their days.

traveler. Some accounts later claimed that sentries fired on the disappearing train, but this did not occur.

Fuller and Murphy knew they had to pursue the train, but there were no other locomotives nearby. At this time Lemuel Kendrick, another conductor, local postmaster, and owner of the hotel, which he leased to the Lacys, appeared. He was dispatched by horse to Marietta, the nearest telegraph, to alert the W&A office.

Fuller, angry and with a deep sense of responsibility, set off down the tracks at a dead run. Murphy and Cain followed. Fireman Anderson chose to remain behind. Passengers and soldiers were shouting and laughing at the spectacle of three men futilely chasing after a speeding train on foot and not even bothering to find horses.

By the time Kendrick reached Marietta and telegraphed the W&A superintendent in Atlanta, the raiders had already cut the line running north. He was told to take the passenger train with the *Pennsylvania*, which he had ordered to hold its departure from Marietta, pick up troops at Camp McDonald, and pursue the *General*. At Big Shanty the less-than-enthusiastic troops took their time loading and the train never departed, not that it could have contributed to the chase owing to the cut track.

William Fuller was running up the tracks as though his life depended on it. The clinging mud between the ties did not slow him.[10] Lagging behind, but not giving up, were Murphy and Cain.

Fuller finally came upon a road gang at Moon's Station. They were still discussing the perplexing sighting of the *General* when Fuller arrived after running 2.5 miles (4 km). They told Fuller that his train had been gone for 30 minutes and that she carried numerous men who had "borrowed" a claw bar. This news gave Fuller pause—maybe there was something more to this story than merely incompetent and scared deserters. He suspected Yankee trickery, but it did not lessen his resolve, although he would now be more cautious.

There were no horses, but there was the section gang's handcar. This was a pole car propelled by men pushing with poles as on a boat in shallow water. There were no hand-pumped cars then but reasonable speeds could be made on level ground and gentle downslopes. It had to be pushed uphill, and on even moderate down-slopes reached dangerous speeds. Murphy and Cain, puffed up and, joined by section gang foreman Bond and a worker, sped off, with Bond and the other man poling while others pushed with their legs. They fully realized they had little chance of catching the *General*, but Fuller was well aware of the *Yonah*, even if he might have to run down to Cooper Iron Works to fetch it. "This in fact was my only hope," he said later. In addition they might be able to find some troops somewhere or even arm themselves.

Fuller and the overcrowded handcar presently came upon the crosstie barricade, and with the section cut out of the wire, it confirmed the train thieves were more than deserters. Manhandling the handcar around the barricade, they continued to Acworth. Here they borrowed two double-barreled shotguns and crowded rifle-armed Martin Rainey and Steven Stokley on to the handcar. Fuller also dispatched a White Smith ahead on horse to raise the alarm, but he gave up and piled on the handcar at Allatoona. They learned more about the wayward train and its strange crew at these two stations. There is no reason given regarding why Fuller didn't commandeer the unidentified yard engine at Allatoona. Perhaps he knew it was unsuited for making any long-distance speed or simply expected additional lifted rails, which the handcar could be manhandled around. On they pushed, but the

10 Tracks were merely laid on tamped ground in those days rather than on elevated rock ballast roadbeds, enhancing drainage.

THE RESOLUTE CONDUCTOR WILLIAM ALLEN FULLER

The *General*'s conductor was born at Morrow Station, Georgia, south of what would become Atlanta, on April 15, 1836 to a cotton-farming family. He had a minimal education in local schools and married Lulu Asher at a young age. She would die in 1872; all their four children tragically died in infancy. Fuller began working for the W&A in September 1855 at 19, his job as a train hand and flagman requiring him to run ahead of trains for miles through winding and hilly countryside to prevent collisions. He was soon made a brakeman, another physically demanding job. The fact that he maintained his fitness was certainly demonstrated a few years later. After just two years of displaying his strong work ethic, skills, and serious take-charge attitude he was promoted to conductor, one of the youngest on the line. This job entailed a wide range of administrative functions: taking tickets, announcing stations, accounting for deliveries and pickups, and maintaining account records.

April 12, 1862 found the almost six-foot Fuller, who was about to turn 29, to be intimately familiar with all aspects of the operation, line, and terrain after seven years of work on the Atlanta–Chattanooga run. He was dedicated to the Southern cause and had attempted to join the militia, but his railroad work was essential and he was prevented from doing so by the governor himself.

Fuller was commended by the state for his valor, determination, and dedication for his actions during the raid and, in August 1863, was made responsible for recruiting and training members of the Independent State Railroad Guard. He served two six-month terms into the summer of 1864 as a captain. From 1870 he worked for the Macon & Western Railroad and returned to the W&A in 1876. He later became a merchant in Atlanta and had remarried in 1874 to Susan Alford, with whom he had five children. Fuller died on December 28, 1905, and is buried in Atlanta's Oakland Cemetery.

While none of the Southern participants in the chase received decorations or monetary awards, Fuller's son was presented a Special Georgia Gold Medal in 1950 commemorating the chase. Fuller was very much aware of his importance in foiling the raiders and he defended his place adamantly when others gave themselves more credit or implied his role was lesser. He just as adamantly pursued the punishment of the raiders and did not approve of their subsequent exchange. Nonetheless he attended the raiders' 1888 reunion and was well received by his former adversaries.

handcar was finally derailed with the men leaping and thrown off where the raiders had lifted the rail outside of Allatoona.[11] Undaunted and uninjured, they were thrilled to see the *Yonah* with a head of steam a mile downslope and across the Etowah River. Fuller sent the rail hand back down the line to summon the next section gang to repair the rail.

The *Yonah* was sitting on its turntable, its loaded tender on a siding. They explained the situation to the *Yonah*'s crew and all hands pitched in, turning the locomotive around, rolling the heavy tender to it, and hitching it up to a flatcar. Murphy oversaw the loading of rails, crossties, and hand tools to repair damage. They also took on several furloughed Confederate soldiers waiting at the station, although these men were probably unarmed. As the old locomotive sped on its way, Fuller was more than confident that he could catch the train thieves with this

---

11 Fuller claims they encountered numerous breaks, but the raiders maintained there was only this one.

"he Raid

"Someone is running with your train!" a startled Anthony Murphy said to conductor James Fuller after sitting down to breakfast in the Lacy Hotel in Big Shanty. It was about 5:30 AM when the raiders rolled off north in full view of Confederate sentries at Camp McDonald across the tracks from the hotel. The baggage and mail car and two passenger cars had been uncoupled from the *General* and left behind. (Pittenger)

powerful engine. The main railyard and junction at Kingston was only 14 miles (23 km) away and the train thieves might get held up there. He was on guard for lifted rails and this held their speed down on curves and rises where forward vision was restricted, but the *Yonah* made, on the whole, excellent progress.

Kingston–Rome Junction

The large town of Carterville was only 2 miles (3 km) beyond Etowah junction. Numerous astonished passengers waited there on the station platform as the *General* sped through without slowing. The raiders again cut the telegraph wire after passing a town. Someone came up with the idea of cutting the wire, fastening it to a boxcar, and driving off ripping down the wire and even the poles.

Five miles (8 km) farther they came upon remote Cass Station—the attendant Cassville town was about 2 miles (3 km) north of the station, as the community had decided it did not want the dirty, noisy railroad running through their town. Here they stocked up on wood and water, oiled the engine, and talked the gullible stationmaster out of the day's time schedule. It was also here that they told their cover story to the stationmaster and tank tender, both of whom accepted it. Andrews, cool under pressure, explained that he was a Confederate officer who had commandeered the train. He was running a load of desperately needed gunpowder to Gen. Beauregard, who was fighting at Corinth, Alabama. This was a weak story at best, as it was known by now that Mitchel had taken Huntsville, and that the Memphis & Charleston RR running west was cut by the Yankees. Fuller assured the stationmaster that the regular passenger train with its usual crew would be along soon. In a way, this was true. They were unable to obtain additional tools for lifting rails, even though they had discreetly enquired. Nor had they obtained any flammable materials necessary to fire bridges. More significantly, it was still raining.

Gen. Mitchel was also doing his part. Having taken Huntsville, he now had access to locomotives and rolling stock on the Memphis & Charleston RR. To the west, toward Confederate-held Corinth, Alabama, he dispatched a train loaded with troops to seize the Tennessee River Bridge at Decatur. This secured his west flank and could take pressure off Buell farther west. He would also send an armed train, followed by troops, 70 miles (113 km) east to Stevenson—this would put him 40 miles (64 km) southwest of Chattanooga. It was hoped to dispatch this train on Friday afternoon,

APRIL 12, 1862

8:30 AM The *General* arrives at the Kingston yard

APRIL 12, 1862

12:30 PM The raiders abandon the *General* and flee into the countryside

The Most Dari...

...***n through Allatoona** Gap. Crossties were natural weathered wood (they were not treated with creosote), 8 inches (20 cm) wide, 8 inches between ties. Rails were fastened to every other tie with one spike on each side (none on alternating ties). There were no sleeper plates, the rail rested directly on ties. Most ties were squared, others were round timbers planed flat on the top side, and ends were saw-cut at an angle. Note that the main line track *(right)* is elevated a few inches higher than sidings *(left)*, standard arrangement so engineers could easily identify the main line alongside sidings. (National Archives)

but delays did not see it on its way until Saturday morning, the same morning the raiders seized the *General*. Aboard the train was the 3rd Division's 9th Brigade, the parent brigade of Andrews' Ohioans. They rolled into Stevenson late Saturday afternoon. If Andrews' expedition had been successful they should have met Mitchel the afternoon of the previous day. Andrews did not know of these latest plans, but this would have to be his destination.

Kingston was only 7 miles (11 km) beyond Cass Station. This was the major railyard between Atlanta and Chattanooga, and the junction with the Rome RR coming in from the west. There were four lengthy sidings on the west side of the main line plus the Rome line branched into a wide "Y" with the two spurs connecting to the main line both north and south. Andrews knew that if there was to be a problem getting through on the line it would be encountered here. He expected at least three trains coming from the north.

The *General* huffed into the Kingston yard at 8:30 AM with the raiders on high alert. Those in the boxcar had their pistols ready and the doors open only a tiny

OTHER PARTICIPATING LOCOMOTIVES

Three other locomotives took part in the great chase to varying degrees, serving in different roles. None of these locomotives remain today as they were scrapped after the war and none were ever photographed.

The *Yonah* (named after the nearby mountain, Cherokee for "bear") has been depicted as a small yard or switch engine in the Walt Disney movie and documentaries. In reality she was a 4-4-0 freight engine built by the Rogers, Ketchum and Grosvenor Locomotive Works, the same firm that built the *General,* and was similar, just older. She did have slightly smaller drive wheels to provide more motive power. She was owned by the W&A, but leased to the Cooper Iron Works. The *Yonah* survived the 1864 Union destruction of the iron works, and after the war served as a stationary engine

providing power at the W&A's Atlanta workshops. She was scrapped at some point, but exactly when has not been recorded.

The *William R. Smith* was an old 4-2-0 locomotive built by the Norris Locomotive Works in Philadelphia. She was operated by the Rome Railroad and named after the line's owner. The *Smith* was transferred to the Muskogee RR on a Columbus-to-Macon, Georgia run. Soon after Appomattox, a Union cavalry raid destroyed her in Columbus.

The final participating locomotive, albeit in a minor role, was the W&A's *Catossa*, named after the northwest Georgia county. She was an older 4-4-0 American Standard.

After being delayed at Kingston for over an hour, Andrews headed north at full speed pushing the *General* hard. This *Harper's* illustration is inaccurate in that most of the raiders remained hidden in a boxcar and they had no shoulder arms.

crack. There were two trains on the sidings (the Rome train and another with an unrecorded engine), yard-crew all about, and, some 200 yards (183 m) northwest of the station, a militia company in the middle of a drill. It was a hive of activity.

The wayward train pulled up just past the station and Andrews strolled confidently up to the station agent, Uriah Stephens, and asked for the switch key. The *General* needed to be on a siding to allow the southbound freight to pass through. He gave the same story about being a powder train under special orders en route to Beauregard and that the regular freight-passenger train would be along presently. Even though many had taken note of the strange train and crew, the raiders were not challenged. Andrews found that the southbound was delayed and the *General* was to wait, so they ran forward on to the northbound line and then backed on to the easternmost siding. There they waited, nervous and alert, but unmolested.

At about 9:00 AM as expected, the awaited *New York* rolled into the yard from the north with over a dozen cars. Andrews approached the conductor, identified himself as a Confederate officer on special assignment, and asked him to clear the main line by moving his train on to a siding. This conductor had no reason to suspect Andrews' authority after noting the respect others in the yard gave him. As the *New York* pulled past, Andrews saw a red flag on the end car. His enquiries uncovered that numerous trains were bringing supplies and rolling stock out of Chattanooga— there would be more unscheduled southbound trains. The reason was because Mitchel was said to have taken Huntsville and was moving toward Chattanooga. The *New York*'s conductor also said he could not get through to Beauregard anyway because of Mitchel's offensive. Andrews, remaining composed and confident, stated that he refused to believe the Yankees were that successful and that he had his orders.

The waiting continued with the men cloistered in the boxcar growing more uneasy having not been kept informed. Just before 10:00 AM a second train arrived. It too carried a red flag warning of yet another train following. Initially, the railroad men at Kingston had readily accepted Andrews' story—anything for the war effort. However, his "special" train had been there for over an hour and Fuller's regular train had not arrived, nor had any telegraph traffic from the south. Why had they not been notified of the special train? Andrews, as cool as ever, responded with anger, declaring that his essential train should be let through, being more important than those fleeing from the north. Finally, Andrews sent Knight back to tell the men in the boxcar the reason for the delay and to remain calm.

The third train finally arrived and Andrews ordered its conductor to move it out of the way. After over an hour's wait the way was clear. However, an old switchman refused

THE CHASE ENDS, 10:00 AM TO 1:30 PM
APRIL 12, 1862

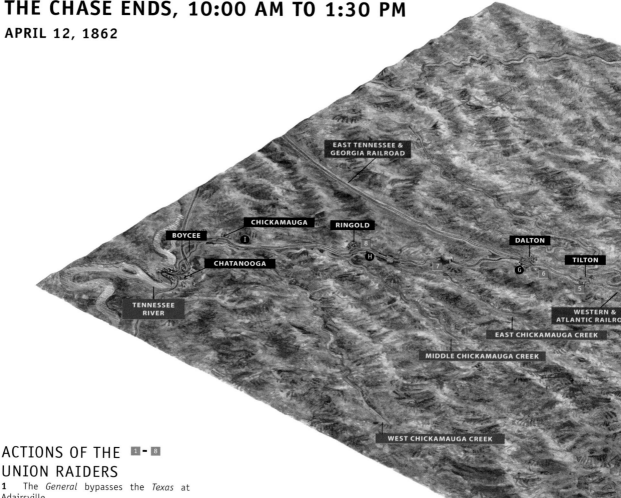

EAST TENNESSEE & GEORGIA RAILROAD

CHICKAMAUGA

BOYCEE

RINGOLD

DALTON

TILTON

CHATANOOGA

TENNESSEE RIVER

WESTERN & ATLANTIC RAILRO

EAST CHICKAMAUGA CREEK

MIDDLE CHICKAMAUGA CREEK

WEST CHICKAMAUGA CREEK

ACTIONS OF THE 1 - 8 UNION RAIDERS

1 The *General* bypasses the *Texas* at Adairsville.

2 The *General* bypasses the *Catoosa* locomotive at Calhoun.

3 The raiders cut the telegraph wire and loosen a rail outside Calhoun. They also detach the boxcar.

4 The raiders begin tossing ties on the track and detach a second boxcar. They are unable to burn the Oostanaula River Bridge.

5 The raiders collect more wood and water for the *General* at Green's Wood Yard and Tilton.

6 The *General* continues towards Chattanooga.

7 The *General* is almost out of fuel and is rapidly loosing steam.

8 The *General* loses power and the raiders are forced to abandon it. They scatter into the forest at 1:00 PM.

ACTIONS OF THE A - I CONFEDERATE PURSUERS:

A Two miles (3 km) south of Adairsville Fuller commandeers the *Texas*.

B The cars of the *Texas* are backed onto the siding in Adairsville and they continue the pursuit.

C The *Texas* picks up a telegraph operator from Dalton. The *Catoosa* follows with 11 soldiers on board.

D Fuller spots his stolen train for the first time. The *Texas* creeps across the loose rail and couples on to a boxcar.

E The *Texas* couples onto a second boxcar.

F The *Texas* detaches two boxcars at Resaca.

G The telegraph operator dropped off at Dalton succeeds in getting a message through to Chattanooga.

H The *Texas* slows as it approaches the abandoned *General*. The *Catoosa* arrives. The *Texas* pulls the *General* back home at 1:30 PM.

I A company of Confederate soldiers from Chattanooga establishes an ambush outside of Chickamauga.

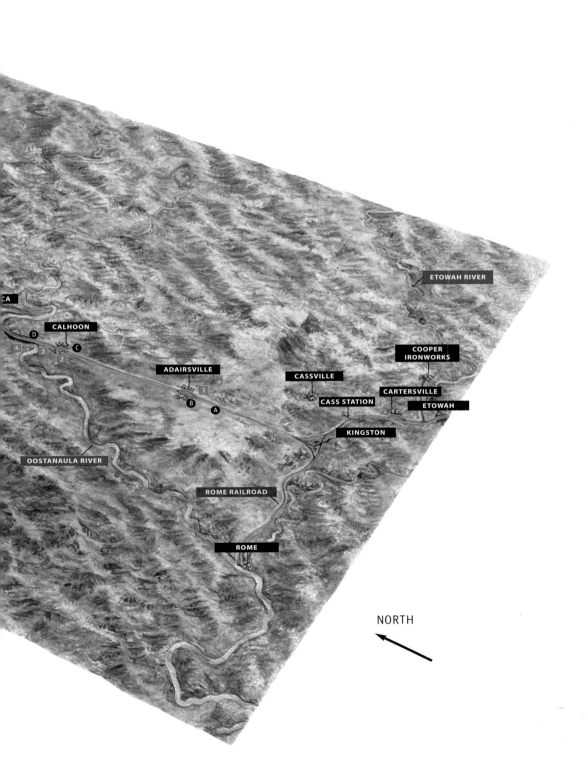

ETOWAH RIVER

CA

CALHOON

D

4 3 2 C

ADAIRSVILLE

1

B

A

CASSVILLE

COOPER
IRONWORKS

CARTERSVILLE

CASS STATION

ETOWAH

KINGSTON

OOSTANAULA RIVER

ROME RAILROAD

ROME

NORTH

Adairsville is the midway point between Atlanta and Chattanooga. It was here that the *Texas*, a southbound freight, was encountered by the raiders. They were further delayed by a second southbound train they had to wait for. Fuller would commandeer the *Texas* two miles (3 km) south of Adairsville. Today the old station, with modern improvements, is the Adairsville Visitor Center and History Museum. (Author)

Andrews' request to open the switch to the main line. Andrews, jesting with the man, took the key, opened the switch enduring threats of arrest, and stepped into the *General*'s cab as it started up the clear line, and departed with the key. It continued to rain.

Fuller, aboard the *Yonah*, was barreling up the line, claiming to have covered the 14 miles (23 km) between Etowah and Kingston in 15 minutes, and this was on a poor track; slowing down through Cartersville, and clearing two barricades. The raiders failed to lift a rail after Etowah because of the lack of tools. They would have had time, were it not for the one-hour delay in Kingston. At Cass Station Fuller heard of Andrews' special powder train story and they now began to worry about an ambush. Fuller rode on the engine's front looking for rail breaks.

Arriving in Kingston, Fuller found the main line and sidings blocked by at least five trains. It would require too much time to shuttle trains about to let the *Yonah* pass; they would have to find another train. Fuller ran to the station and explained the situation. The telegraph line north was already cut and the *General* had departed only minutes before. Amid the confusion Fuller ran to the *William R. Smith*, the Rome RR engine, and explained to the engineer that he needed his locomotive. In the meantime Murphy had the *New York* drop its cars and was coupling on the flatcar of repair supplies as it was the better engine. The *Smith* dropped its one passenger car, retaining its baggage car, which was promptly boarded by the militia company, who were partaking of corn liquor amidst all the excitement. Murphy sent a runner to tell Fuller to move the *Smith* and saw that engine pulling out with Wiley Harbin at the throttle, William Kernodle stoking, and Joe Lassiter working the brakes. Murphy raced after it, abandoning the ready *New York*, and barely caught up.

Outside of Kingston the *General* halted, erected a barricade, and tore the wire down. There was no further concern about maintaining the schedule. Andrews was pushing the *General* at top speed. They halted again 6 miles (10 km) north to lift a rail.[12] Half the men worked on the rail with their one tool and others loaded ties to fuel bridge fires; spare ties were stacked at intervals along the line.[13] The rail was only partly loosened when they were stunned to hear a train whistle. This spurred the

---

12 Barricades were constructed by jamming two crossties in an X-form between crossties and under the rails. Others were erected by haphazardly stacking ties, branches, and fence poles. There was no time to make "Sherman's bowties" by heating lifted rails and bending them around telegraph poles or trees.

13 Crossties were usually oak and were not treated with creosote or tar and turpentine at this time.

men to yank up the rail with such force that it snapped. They boarded with the rail and were off at top speed. Ahead was Adairsville, where they would have to pass two more southbound trains. They had to make it to the Oostanaula River Bridge some 20 miles (32 km) ahead, but they had little chance now unless it and some of the Chickamauga bridges were burned.

At Adairsville, the midway point between Atlanta and Chattanooga, Andrews found the *Texas*, the southbound freight with 21 cars. Andrews presented his usual story, convincing the conductor to continue south and clear the line for him. The following southbound passenger train was 30 minutes overdue. Cautioned to go slow and send a flagman ahead on curves, Andrews headed out. He took neither precaution other than keeping the whistle going while running at top speed. They reached over 60 mph (97 km per hour) by dousing oil into the firebox.

Tearing into Calhoun, they narrowly avoided colliding with the passenger train pulled by the *Catoosa*. She quickly backed up enough to let the *General* careen on to the siding, but the raiders had to screech to a stop as the long freight train blocked the siding's exit. Rattled by the near collision the *Catoosa*'s crew was hardly cooperative with the reckless "special" train. An equally shaken Andrews told his story, but the angry crew was reluctant and feared another northbound train would be heading in their direction. Finally Andrews, using his typical bluster, ordered the crew to move the train forward. The next step would have been to draw pistols. With no more scheduled southbound trains, and the broken rail between them and the pursuing train, there was nothing to stop them.

It was not long before the *William R. Smith* was halted by the rail break. Murphy was glad to be rid of the underpowered engine and the drunken militiamen. Fuller and Murphy took off at a run, knowing the passenger train with the *Texas* was heading toward them. In the meantime the *Smith*'s engineer, Harbin, removed a rail from behind his train and replaced the broken rail. They went on in hopes of being of aid. Two miles (3 km) outside of Adairsville, Fuller and Murphy met the *Texas*, related their story, and started backing to Adairsville. The cars were backed on to a siding; the *Texas* pulled forward, and then started backing up the main line. There was no way to turn around, or a need to. She would run just as fast in reverse as forward. This newest W&A locomotive was fresh out of overhaul and easily equal to the *General*. Engineer Peter Bracken, assisted by fireman Henry Haney and wood-passer Alonzo Martin, opened her up.

Running at over 50 mph (80 km per hour), the *Texas* charged up the track with Fuller hanging off the tender's side to give him more of a view around curves. They

Unable to lift rails rapidly enough and with the crossties barricades failing to delay the *Texas* sufficiently, the raiders battered holes through the ends of the boxcars and desperately tossed crossties on to the tracks in a futile effort to derail or at least slow the *Texas*. Most of the crossties simply bounced off the tracks owing to the *General's* high speed. (Pittenger) slowed enough at Calhoun to pass word of the situation and took aboard Edward Henderson, the Dalton telegraph operator who had come down on the *Catoosa* searching for the apparent wire break. They also took on Fleming Cox as a second fireman. The *Catoosa* followed the *Texas* out of Calhoun after dropping its cars. Piling on to the tender were Capt W.J. Whitsitt and ten troopers of the 1st Georgia Infantry. They had been bound south and had convinced engineer Joe Renard at gunpoint to join them. Thus the final phase of the Great Locomotive Chase commenced.

The great chase

The *General* halted 1.5 miles (2 km) north of Calhoun, where the raiders cut the wire, loosened a rail, and loaded crossties for bridge-burning fuel. The freshly oiled *General* was still in top running order, but low on wood and water. As they struggled with the rail, they again heard a train whistle and saw the *Texas* barreling toward them in reverse. Leaving the wedged-up bent rail they frantically boarded and flew off, but detached a boxcar around the curve in hopes of causing a collision. It was a mystery to the raiders where the train came from or how they had been alerted with the rail and wire cut. This was the first point at which Andrews could have ambushed his pursuers, but chose not to—he was, after all, more used to talking his way out of trouble rather than shooting his way out.

Ahead Fuller saw his train for the first time since its theft and he was surprised to see so many Yankees scrambling aboard. The *Texas* was able to creep across the loosened rail, but their slow speed prevented them from ramming the boxcar, which was un-braked, undamaged, and loaded with ties and brush—obviously bridge-burning

THE *TEXAS*

The *Texas*, the main locomotive participating in the great chase, was also an American Standard and a 4-4-0. In fact she and the *General* were quite similar in design and capabilities. The *Texas* was built in Paterson, New Jersey, as was the *General*. The *Texas*, however, was built by Danforth, Cooke and Company for $9,050 in 1856 and it too had 5 ft. (1.5 m) driver wheels. The *Texas* suffered no damage during the chase and saw further service for several years afterwards. In 1863 she was sent to Virginia to exchange firewood for much-needed salt, which was scarce in Georgia, and was returned to the W&A in 1866. She was renamed the *Cincinnati* in 1880 and was leased by the Nashville, Chattanooga & St. Louis RR in 1890 until, at nearly fifty years old, the warhorse was finally taken out of service in 1903.

The retired *Texas* was a much different locomotive than the pursuer of the *General*. Her boilers had been replaced twice, she was converted to a coal burner in the early 1870s like the *General*, and in 1886 the 60-inch (152 cm) drive wheels were replaced by 56-inch (142 cm) wheels to provide a little more traction power. The

locomotive was deteriorating on a yard siding and a campaign commenced in 1907 to save the *Texas* from the scrapyard. She was moved to Grant Park in Atlanta in 1911, and finally moved into the Cyclorama Building in the park. In 1936 she was finally restored to much as she appeared when she was acquired by the W&A, although the smaller drivers were retained. 1973 saw the *Texas* entered on the National Register of Historic Places and she remains on public display in the Cyclorama Building (commemorating the Battle for Atlanta).

Road Numbering: It should be noted that some depictions of the *General* and *Texas* during the chase show them bearing locomotive numbers on their boiler sandboxes. Road numbers were not assigned to W&A locomotives until 1866. The *General* was assigned "39" and then "3" in about 1882. The *Texas* was numbered "49" and then "12" when she was renamed the *Cincinnati* in 1880. In 1890 she was renumbered "212." The first numbers assigned were in the order that the locomotives were acquired by the W&A. At the time of the chase they were identified only by nameplates on the sides of their boilers.

Desperately low of wood fuel, the raiders began ripping wood from the remaining boxcar to stoke the *General*'s firebox. They also attempted to start a fire in the boxcar before dropping it off to block the *Texas*, an attempt that failed. (Pittenger)

fuel. The near-level grade here did not give the kicked-back boxcar enough speed to be dangerous. Coupling it to the tender with Fuller on top as lookout and brakeman, they sped on.

The raiders in the last of the two boxcars battered a hole through the end with a crosstie. They began tossing ties out to block the rail, but most bounced a considerable distance owing to their speed. This only slowed the *Texas* slightly as two men ran alongside clearing the ties. Andrews believed there were more than just the seven, mostly unarmed, men aboard his pursuer. They dropped the second boxcar just before a Chickamauga Creek bridge. Its brakes were not set, nor was it derailed as the chasers feared. One of the many myths surrounding the chase was that this car was set ablaze and left on a covered bridge. Many of the surviving raiders claimed this, but it was not so, though they may have attempted to fire it. The *Texas* simply coupled on the second boxcar and sped on. Another myth is that the pursuers fired on the fleeing *General*, but this too never occurred. There is debate about how adamantly the raiders pushed for Andrews to ambush the pursuers. Some claim they strongly urged it and that he may well have considered it, but apparently he felt the pursuers were present in well-armed numbers. The raiders, with every intention of firing the 840-foot-long (256 m) covered Oostanaula River Bridge (river 230 foot [70 m] wide), were forced to leave the rain-soaked structure undamaged as they roared through nearby Resaca. Fuller deposited the two boxcars on a siding there. From this point on the increasingly hilly terrain made the line even more winding and there were numerous covered bridges over Chickamauga Creek and its branches. This was the chase's turning point—the Yankee raiders were now alarmed and in flight.

Both engines shrieked northward on the rough winding track, throwing all caution and good judgment to the wind. More ties were hurled from the remaining boxcar and the *Texas* would alternately fall behind and then gain ground. Wood was running out aboard the *General*. "Alf" Wilson stated, "We crammed the furnace with every combustible we could…" With wheels spinning in reverse, the *General* ran into Green's Wood Station outside of Tilton and the men frantically tossed wood into the tender. At Tilton, water was poured into the tender and they sped off with it still gushing, as the *Texas* was almost atop them.

The *General* had to slow down in the Dalton yard, ensuring they did not inadvertently switch on to the northeast branch line to Cleveland, Tennessee, rather than head to Chattanooga. Andrews ran into the station making his customary demand and ensured the switch was correctly turned. The passage of the junction yard at high speed was a harrowing experience, with the boxcar almost overturning on a left turn.

The *Texas* followed just minutes behind. Telegrapher Henderson leapt off at Dalton and hammered out Fuller's handwritten message to Brig. Gen. Danville Leadbetter, the former catcher of bridge-burners, in Chattanooga: "My train was captured this a.m. at Big Shanty, evidently by federal soldiers in disguise. They are making rapidly for Chattanooga, possibly with the idea of burning RR bridges in their rear. If I do not capture them in the meantime, see that they do not pass Chattanooga."

At the same time the raiders tore down the wire 2 miles (3 km) past the junction town. They were moments too late—Henderson's message went through. The raiders would have found a hot reception 27 miles (43 km) ahead. Leadbetter dispatched a company[14] by train from Chattanooga to establish an ambush 11 miles (17 km) south, just past Chickamauga Station. In a railroad cut they lifted rails and the company took up firing positions on both sides with a lookout posted ahead. No matter what happened now, the raiders' fate was sealed.

Chetoogeta Mountain loomed 8 miles (13 km) ahead of the raiders. Tunnel Hill, lined with brick and limestone blocks, ran 1,447 feet (441 m) as it cut through the mountain. The *General* blasted through the dark tunnel at top speed. The soldiers being bounced around in the boxcar were hoping they would halt to set an ambuscade. Instead, Andrews pressed on.

Fuller wisely slowed the *Texas*, concerned at just such an occurrence, and looked for obstructions. The dim light leaking from the far end caused the rails to reflect a shine, making it possible to detect crossties and breaks but there were none. Murphy noticed there was little heavy smoke hanging in the tunnel; the *General* was low on steam. Emerging into the open, the *Texas* poured on speed, passing through Tunnel Hill town.

The *General* remained in the lead but her engine crew were exhausted. There was barely any wood or water left and they were out of oil. Wood scraps, caps, even

THE GEORGIA MILITIA

The various state military forces went through a convoluted series of reorganizations and call-ups for Confederate active service. A bewildering array of different organizations was formed through the war. Much of the turmoil was due to Governor Joseph E. Brown's meddling and disputes with Jefferson Davis' government on the right of states to raise and control armed forces. These forces came to be known as "Joe Brown's Pets."

The first such state troops, the Georgia Army or "Secession Regiments" and then the 4th Brigade, Georgia Volunteers, were called up and eventually placed under Confederate control. The Georgia State Troops were established next, mainly for coastal defense.

In early 1862 the 14 counties in extreme northwest Georgia comprised the 12th Division of the Georgia Militia. It was divided, by county, into 1st and 2nd Brigades. This is where most of the fleeing raiders were captured. Militia divisions and brigades were purely administrative organizations and were nowhere close to those formations in strength and capabilities, essentially being collections of town companies. Counties were divided into militia districts in which a 63-man company was supposed to be raised from able

members enrolled by appointed captains. These companies could, in reality, be much smaller or larger. They were to be organized into battalions and regiments, but these existed only on paper.

The militiamen chasing the raiders through the Georgia hills were part-time volunteers, what would today be called "weekend warriors." They typically met on a Saturday once a month where it was doubtful that much military instruction took place. This day was selected as men brought their families into town and attended church the next day. If called up for state duty, such as chasing bridge burners or guarding bridges, they might be given "agricultural leave" during planting and harvest seasons.

Other than possibly the elected officers, few if any of the militiamen possessed uniforms, wearing only homespun garb. There were no cavalry units, but some men in a given unit possessed horses. They provided their own weapons, which were mostly muzzle-loading double-barreled shotguns, squirrel guns, and deer rifles of varied makes. Walt Disney's image of gray-coated cavalrymen in all their gallant splendor chasing the raiders as they fled the *General* was purely imagined glamour.

---

14 "Moccasin Rangers"—no other unit identification available.

The 840-foot-long (256 m) covered Oostanaula River Bridge was of timber trestle construction in 1862. It was much later replaced by a modern concrete bridge, but the original south end abutments are still an integral portion of the bridge. (Allen Shoppe)

Andrews' saddlebags went into the firebox. The men in the boxcar had jettisoned their last tie. They attempted to fire the remaining boxcar with a shovel of coals. The rain-wet car refused to blaze and the smoke drove the men on to the tender. They rumbled through Ringgold 7 miles (11 km) up the line and then made it around a curve another 1.3 miles (2 km) before the *General* gave out on an upgrade. The *Texas* was barreling at them, but reduced speed when it became apparent the chase was slowing as they feared the Yankees might reverse the engine into them. Andrews hastily discussed options with the engine crew and then directed, "Scatter in small parties and escape the best way you can." Rather than the stand and fight to the death promised by Andrews six days earlier, it was now every man for himself.

It was just before 12:30 PM—the 88-mile (142 km) chase had lasted a little over six hours.

The end of the line

Fuller charged into the woods after the locomotive thieves, shotgun in hand. Murphy raced to the *General*. He found it virtually undamaged but out of wood and what

The stone- and brick-lined confines of the original tunnel are shown here in this southward-looking view from just inside the north portal. Fuller was concerned about an ambush awaiting him at this end or that crossties may have been dropped on the track. There was no time to stop and light the headlamp. (Allen Shoppe)

little was left still smoldering in the firebox. The *Catoosa* soon arrived and the soldiers rushed into the trees amid the drizzle. They soon found themselves dead-ended on a ridge, where one accidentally shot himself—the only shot fired and the single casualty of the entire affair. About half an hour after being abandoned, the *Texas* coupled on the *General*'s boxcar and towed the locomotive back home.

It did not take long for word to spread that Yankee train stealers and spies were running loose in the hills, most heading northwest and others northeast. Andrews' one-day delay meant that this Saturday was drill day for the militia. Hundreds of part-time soldiers and civilians armed with their own weapons spread out through the countryside with the aim of becoming heroes. Most were afoot, others on plow horses and mules. They loosed their dogs and were bent on revenge and sport.

The renegades stood little chance. They had not eaten since the evening before, were unprovisioned, unequipped, and had no idea where they were. The local hunters were familiar with the rugged terrain and, in spite of the rain, wildly enthusiastic. Some of the evaders linked up in larger groups. All were tired, soaked, and lost. The track may have run north but, as winding as it was, striking out perpendicular from a given point did not mean one was traveling west. The terrain was so broken and densely wooded that in order to make any headway the evaders eventually had to take to trails and roads, and this is where most were caught wandering aimlessly. Some intentionally fled in the "wrong" direction hoping to elude pursuers and then find the Tennessee River and follow it west to Union lines. Even though the alarm had been raised, some men were able to beg shelter and food from remote locals.

Andrews, who had a compass, traveling with Marion Ross and John Wollam, almost made it to friendly territory, being captured just 12 miles (19 km) from Union-occupied Bridgeport. "Alf" Wilson and Mark Wood, traveling part-way by stolen boat on the Tennessee, were picked up near Stevenson, which had by then been abandoned by the Federals. Every raider was captured within days.

When captured, many gave the Kentucky regiment story, saying they were from Flemingsburg, Kentucky. Word of the story had spread, and repeating it gave them away. They were not treated any more roughly than expected, although this was harsh enough, with mobs screaming for their lynching. Jacob Parrott, however, was severely whipped. All were clapped in irons when caught. Most were taken to Ringgold, then Camp McDonald, where the chase had begun, and all ended up in the Marietta jail.

The two late sleepers, Martin Hawkins and John Porter, were still outside Marietta. Considering their position and that the train had been stolen, they decided to walk to Camp McDonald and enlist. They were voted into the 9th Georgia Infantry Battalion, but their service under "Stars and Bars" was brief. Apparently a captured raider revealed that two men had been left in Marietta and then word circulated of

OVERLEAF
After 88 miles (142 km) of cutting rails and wire, duping stationmasters and erecting barricades, the six-hour chase was over. Out of fuel and water, the 20 raiders abandoned the *General* just north of Ringgold, still many miles from their intended destination. It was every man for himself as they sprinted into the Georgia hills. The pursuing *Texas* slowed as William Fuller approached the stalled *General*, fearing that the Yankee raiders might attempt to reverse the locomotive into him, but there was no steam left for such an attempt. With the militia alerted and many enthusiastic civilians turning out to assist in the search for the engine thieves, the raiders were all rounded up within days.

Ringgold Depot today serves as the town's museum. It was rebuilt after the war, having been destroyed by Union troops during the 1864 Atlanta Campaign. The original stone walls can be seen. It was here that the first militiamen, attending their Saturday drill, were dispatched to hunt down the fleeing raiders. Most were first brought here after their capture. (Allen Shoppe)

At Green's Wood Station outside of Tilton the raiders frenziedly flung wood into the *General*'s tender knowing the *Texas* was not far behind. Despite the full load pictured here, they were only able to fill the tender with less than a quarter of its capacity before they were forced to move out. (Pittenger)

the Kentucky story. They were questioned, arrested, and, after calls for their lynching, joined their comrades in irons.

The newspapers gloated over the foiled engine thieves' plot and the capture of the spies, especially their leader, whom the Atlanta *Daily Intelligencer* described as: "a Yankee scoundrel, but reckless and daring."

Promoted to major general in recognition of his successes, even though he never took Chattanooga, Mitchel consolidated his position and his under-strength division was dispersed, occupying towns and guarding the rail line. Neither Buell nor Halleck provided reinforcements as they had their own objectives. Mitchel had to content himself with sitting still and fighting off Confederate cavalry raids. He made no official mention of the failed Chattanooga Railroad Expedition in dispatches, although he was aware of the raiders' fate via smuggled Atlanta newspapers.

The point 1.3 miles (2 km) north of Ringgold, and 88 miles (142 km) from Big Shanty, where the General ground to a halt after running out of steam and the raiders scattered in all directions. As on the day of the chase it was raining. The raiders' names and units are included at the plaque's bottom portion. (Allen Shoppe)

THE RAIDERS' FATE

Called spies, villains, and train thieves by Southern newspapers, within days the 20 raiders were transferred to the Chattanooga jail. They were under the charge of a despicable jailer named Swims, a drunken, uncouth individual who passed his sober moments harassing the prisoners. The small two-story brick building was surrounded by a wooden stockade. Entry was via exterior stairs to the second floor, which contained a holding cell and the jailer's squalid quarters. The ground floor was reached by a ladder through a trapdoor and held a small kitchen and the filthy inmates' cell. The "Hole," as it was known, had also served as a jail for runaway slaves.

Andrews and others were personally interrogated by Brig. Gen. Leadbetter and all were accused of being Yankee spies. The widely known Andrews made no effort to conceal his identity and a considerable amount of Confederate money was taken off him. Even though they had failed and caused no real damage, there was little doubt they

All of the raiders were captured within days of the failed raid. Shackled, they were marched through towns with crowds shouting for the immediate hanging of the "engine stealers." (Pittenger)

would be court-martialed as spies. The prisoners considered all manner of escape plans, but it was virtually hopeless owing to the strength of the jail building and the guards.

Pittenger and "Alf" Wilson took the lead in planning their defense. They would maintain they were merely U.S. Army soldiers performing a military operation. They had not sneaked through Confederate pickets, lurked about encampments, or attempted to gain any information to pass back to their commander. They were to capture a train and destroy bridges—military targets—in support of their unit's advance. During the trial they would further argue that Confederate raiders habitually lacked uniforms and were treated as prisoners of war. They all agreed not to reveal anything of Andrews' rumored spying efforts, his earlier postponed raid, who had served as the engineer, and that Campbell was a civilian claiming he was in Company K, 2nd Ohio. There was no escaping the fact that they had volunteered for a secret expedition behind enemy lines, wore civilian clothes, and deceived Southerners about their identity. The newspapers were outraged at the train thieves and were soon calling it the "great railroad chase." But at the same time they exhibited a grudging admiration for the audacity and boldness of the devious raiders.

Andrews, the mastermind, was tried first. His known background worked against him and there was little question that he would be branded a spy. He did argue that he attacked no Southerners, had not intended to burn bridges, had been a member of the Kentucky State Guard (a dubious claim that was intended to afford him a measure of military status), and had been pressed into performing service for the Union. Regardless, he was found guilty of spying and treason since he had conducted business in good faith in the Confederacy.

Accusations that they had "stolen" the locomotive were countered by claims that they "captured" it, and not deep behind the front lines, but immediately adjacent to a Confederate force. Such arguments fell on deaf ears.

Pittenger, probably because he had been so articulate and argued their case, was often segregated from the other prisoners and given some preferential treatment, much to the annoyance of the others. It was not long before some accused him of cooperating with the enemy to save himself.

On May 1, the prisoners were suddenly removed from the Hole and loaded on a train for Atlanta, pulled by none other than the *General*. Mitchel was moving on Chattanooga. They could not help but notice the much increased presence of bridge and station guards and the passport system. The next day they went on to Madison, 70 miles (113 km) east of Atlanta. But Mitchel's "advance" had been nothing more than a move to secure his supply lines and the prisoners were sent back to Swims' hellhole three days later, although they were incarcerated on the more tolerable second floor.

On May 31, 12 raiders—Brown, Buffum, Campbell, Knight, Mason, Pittenger, Robertson, Ross, Scott, Shadrach, Slavens, and George Wilson—were transported to Knoxville, Kentucky for trial. That same day, Andrews was given his death warrant to be executed on June 7. The only way Andrews could be saved was to escape. The nine prisoners began planning for their leader's getaway. They miraculously managed

The horrid Chattanooga Jail, also known as the "Negro Jail" or "Swims Jail" after its malicious and unsavory turnkey or simply the "Hole." The prisoners were housed on the airless, squalid ground floor. The door on the ground floor was for the separate kitchen. James Andrews and John Wollam managed to escape a week before Andrews' execution. They made a hole through the bricks under the roof's eaves; having been moved to the second floor. Both were recaptured and Andrews was executed as scheduled. (Pittenger)

to bust Andrews and Wollam out and they made it over the stockade with sentries blasting away. The two were separated and Andrews lost his boots. Wollam eluded his trackers, found a canoe on the Tennessee River, and paddled west. Andrews made it only 12 miles (19 km) and was recaptured two days later, half dead.

In Knoxville only seven of the 12 raiders were tried, one a day: Campbell, Robertson, Ross, Scott, Shadrach, Slavens, and George Wilson. The conclusion was essentially predetermined. On June 14, all were sentenced "to be hung [*sic*] by the neck until he is dead."

On the day of Andrews' execution, June 7, he and the other raiders were quickly evacuated to Atlanta as the 3rd Division was again attacking Chattanooga's outskirts. Andrews was taken to a gallows on the north side of Atlanta. But the public hanging

JUNE 7, 1862

Andrews executed

JUNE 18, 1862

Seven of the raiders executed at the Atlanta Graveyard

Access to the jail's ground-floor dungeon was via a ladder from the second floor, which was pulled up after letting prisoners in or out. Much of the time the prisoners were shackled together. There was barely enough room for all to lie on the dirt floor to sleep. (Pittenger)

The June 18, 1862, execution in the Atlanta Graveyard of raiders Campbell, Robertson, Ross, Scott, Shadrach, Slavens, and George Wilson. Wilson, to the right, made a brief speech maintaining they were only soldiers doing their duty. (Pittenger)

was botched—when the platform dropped, his feet struck the ground. One guard shouldered him off the ground so that he was strangled. The crowd, which included William Fuller, was appalled. The spy was buried at the site.

The remaining eight prisoners from Chattanooga were incarcerated in the Fulton County Jail in Atlanta. They were soon joined by the 12 from Knoxville and all began plotting their escape. On June 18, a detail appeared and announced that the seven condemned prisoners were to be immediately executed. They were taken by cart to the Atlanta Graveyard (today's Oakland Cemetery). In spite of the lack of announcement, a crowd formed and Fuller was once again present. Mounting the gallows, George Wilson gave a moving speech regarding their fate and said that they had simply performed their duty. The platform dropped and two of the ropes snapped, letting Campbell and Stevens fall to the ground. The ropes were replaced and they were hanged an hour later. Even the guards were aghast, much less the civilian spectators. In desperation, the remaining 13 raiders sent a letter to Confederate President Jefferson Davis begging for mercy. There was no response.

At the end of the month the prisoners were surprised when John Wollam walked into the cell, having finally been recaptured after his escape with Andrews. In mid-August they sent another letter to Maj. Gen. Baxton Bragg. Some argued against this course of action, as they appeared to have been "forgotten," and this was better than facing the certainty of no reprieve. It was eventually forwarded to Davis who inquired if there was "a discrimination between these and the others who were executed for the same offense." Enquiries went back down through the official channels. The other prisoners had not been yet been tried nor sentenced. No one knew what to do. Back in their Union units the men were reported as either being on "detached duty," "secret service," or "special duty." Some were assumed to have been executed but no one, least of all their families, had any direct knowledge of their fate.

They planned to make a break on October 14, but rains postponed this until the 16th. A few other Union prisoners would accompany them, although they would not release civilian criminals. At dinnertime some forced their way out of their cell and surrounded the jailer, accompanied only by two sympathetic black servants. They opened the other cells, burst into the courtyard, and caught the guards by surprise. There was a general melee and shots were fired. No one was hit, but Buffum, Parrott, Pittenger, and Reddick were caught as the others made it over the wall and ran for the woods. One of the escaping Tennesseans was recaptured, and a Confederate deserter they released was eventually caught and hanged. Raiders Bensinger and Mason were caught within two days.

Amazingly, even with cries of "Don't take one of the villains alive" and the alarm raised, eight raiders made good their escape and undertook incredible adventures to secure their freedom, sometimes aided by Union sympathizers. "Alf" Wilson and Wood floated south down the Chattanooga and Apalachicola rivers to the Gulf of Mexico, where they were picked up by a Union blockade ship on November 7. Porter and Wollam went west-northwest, making Corinth, Mississippi on November 18. Dorsey and Hawkins headed north to Lebanon, Kentucky, reaching there on the same date, while Brown and Knight, also moving north, reached Somerset, Kentucky, on December 2. All eventually rejoined their units.

Bensinger, Buffum, Mason, Parrott, Pittenger, and Reddick remained jailed and fearful of swift revenge. However, in the early days of December they were informed that they were to be part of a prisoner exchange and were sent to Richmond, Virginia. Here, protracted negotiations took place before they finally went home with other exchanged prisoners on March 17, 1863. They too returned to their units.

All returned raiders survived the war, although some were wounded. Most

received promotions and seven were awarded officer commissions. Brown, Mason, Porter, Wollam, and Wood were again captured during the Battle of Chickamauga. All were exchanged or escaped except Wollam. He was recognized as an escaped raider and imprisoned until he escaped again before the war's end.

In July 12, 1862, President Lincoln approved the Medal of Honor, the Army's first and only medal for valor. When it was learned that many of the raiders had survived and returned, it was suggested that their exploits were suitable for the first presentations of the decoration. Most of the raiders, including those who had been executed, would receive the Medal of Honor, but there were exceptions. Andrews and Campbell were ineligible, being civilians. Even Hawkins and Porter, who overslept, attempted to join a Confederate unit, and were discovered and imprisoned, received the award. Llewellyn and Smith had been forced to join a Confederate unit en route. Llewellyn escaped, but Smith was jailed for disloyalty and later escaped. Neither received the award, until Smith's father lobbied for its presentation to his son and it was granted. The executed Shadrach and George Wilson were never presented the award posthumously. It is not known why, other than perhaps they were overlooked. Their relatives never made an issue of it.

The raiders held occasional reunions, the last being in 1906.

On October 16, 1862, the raiders surprised their guards in the Fulton County Jail in Atlanta and Brown, Dorsey, Hawkins, Knight, Porter, "Alf" Wilson, Wollam, and Wood made good their escape. Bensinger, Buffum, Mason, Parrott, Pittenger, and Reddick failed to make it out of the compound or were caught within two days. They were all later exchanged. (Pittenger)

ANALYSIS

OCTOBER 16, 1862

Eight raiders escape from Fulton County Jail in Atlanta

The Chattanooga Railroad Expedition was a bold, if relatively minor, effort in terms of the expenditure of manpower and resources. Two civilians, 22 soldiers, and several thousand dollars were expended on an operation that had the potential of contributing a great deal to Gen. Mitchel's comparatively small-scale effort to seize Chattanooga. Its success would have contributed significantly to the campaign and possibly helped shorten the war, but its failure did not cause or even adversely affect the campaign's attempt to achieve its goal. This, perhaps, is why Mitchel was willing to launch the raid. It would benefit him if successful, but the success of his campaign did not hinge on the success or failure of Andrews' mischief. That might be a valuable lesson for modern-day mission planners.

One point is that if Andrews had been able to burn W&A bridges and close the line for days if not weeks, but was foiled in the final stages, it would still have aided Mitchel. However, he would not even have been aware of any success until after the fact, either because of the lack of rail traffic arriving in Chattanooga, through smuggled newspapers, or from knowledgeable and talkative prisoners. Even with modern technology, the same could occur today if there was a communications failure. It has been assessed that if Andrews had succeeded, Mitchel could have taken Chattanooga in five days.

It is easy to judge the mistakes and flaws of a mission plan and its execution with the benefit of hindsight—one should temper any criticism with that in mind. There were mistakes made by both the pursuers and the pursued, but it can be said for the most part they made reasonable decisions in the heat of the moment in view of the information they possessed.

The most significant flaw was Andrews' reluctance to set an ambush or avoid directly confronting groups with force. The first was the road crew at Moon's Station. It is not recorded how many men were present, maybe 8–12, possibly fewer. Apparently, there was no one else nearby and they were, of course, unarmed and unaware of any danger. Rather than keeping up the charade as legitimate railroaders and "borrowing" a single claw bar, the raiders should have drawn their revolvers and taken all the tools (as well as their lunch). This would have given them the essential tools and the only damage done would have been to tip off Fuller that the locomotive thieves were organized and armed earlier than he later realized. Having these tools would have allowed them to remove rails completely in a matter of minutes, and this would have precluded further pursuit. Realistically, it would be expecting too much for Andrews to have the foresight to destroy the handcar.

The second mistake was at Etowah when Andrews decided to leave the *Yonah* undamaged. This provided Fuller with a locomotive. There were not many Southerners present and the few soldiers were unarmed. The *Yonah* could have been destroyed simply by opening the throttle, with the engineer leaping off and sending it at full speed down the 2.5-mile (4 km) dead-end spur, the direction it was facing.

Failing to steal more tools or disabling the *Yonah*, Andrews' reluctance to set an ambush was a significant miscalculation. There is nothing in Andrews' background indicating he had ever used force or was ever involved in gunplay. His experience and nature was to talk his way out of situations. Lacking military experience he balked at the idea of direct attack.

There were several opportunities to set an ambush: the exit of Tunnel Hill is the most often discussed, but this was rather obvious. An earlier ambush would have been more certain. The *General* could have halted around a curve and waited as the

MARCH 17, 1863

The remaining seven raiders are exchanged for Confederate prisoners

The restored *Texas* today in the Cyclorama Building, Grant Park in Atlanta. (Allen Shoppe)

raiders set the ambush but there would have been a danger of the pursuing locomotive, with the cab crew gunned down, speeding into the rear of the waiting *General*. However, a close-range barrage of almost 20 .36-cal and .44-cal six-guns blasting into the *Texas'* wooden cab would have been devastating.

Andrews' intelligence collection for the mission was exceptional. He knew the regular train schedules, and where telegraph stations, woodyards, water towers, and other facilities were; was familiar with W&A routines and with the necessary switches; had spied out military units; and was familiar with the local situation (he was known to have visited the *Southern Confederacy* reading room in Atlanta). He slipped up only by not considering the monthly militia drill date.

Andrews' unilateral decision for a one-day delay was another factor contributing to failure, although it could not be helped owing to the unexpected incessant rains that slowed the raiders' infiltration. Another flaw was providing the same Kentucky regiment cover story to every man, which exposed many raiders.

The first presentations of the Army's newly established Medal of Honor were to the Andrews' raiders.

Materially, Andrews was poorly prepared. It would not have been possible to bring railroad hand tools, but he failed to aggressively obtain them. He could have brought a couple of wire-cutters for telegraph wires. The raiders had no food or water, no maps, other than possibly one in Andrews' saddlebags; they had poor clothing for cool or wet weather, and only Andrews possessed a compass. He was overly confident on making his timely rendezvous west of Chattanooga.

The raiders could not have carried tins of coal oil (kerosene) aboard, but Andrews could have hidden a supply at an identifiable point outside a town. However, this would have required significant effort and time to prepare. They used up their machine oil by necessity on the *General* and the remainder thrown into the firebox. There is no mention of using the whale oil or coal oil in the *General's* headlamp.

In many ways the Andrews Raid was more of a benefit to the South than the North. There was little physical damage; no bridges, locomotives, or rolling stock were damaged, other than some easily repaired holes knocked through three boxcars. The few lifted rails and cut wires were repaired before the day was done. The momentary disruption of the W&A schedule and some confusion had no significant impact on military operations. It did provide welcome excitement and gave the militia some exercise and material for tall tales. There were, of course, some damaged reputations, bruised egos, and shake-ups among the authorities.

Having "borrowed" a claw bar from a section gang at Moon's Station, the raiders lifted a rail to halt pursuers. The lack of adequate tools made this a slow and labor-intensive job and would eventually lead to the foiling of the raid. At the same time the telegraph wire was cut. (Pittenger)

The first newspaper account of the chase, appearing in the April 15, 1862 issue of the Atlanta *Southern Confederacy*, stated: "Let this be a warning to the railroad men and every body else in the Confederate States. Let an engine never be left alone a moment. Let additional guards be placed on our bridges. This is a matter we urged in the Confederacy long ago. We hope it will now be heeded."

Indeed, the biggest benefit to the South was a boost to internal security. Bridge and station guards were increased and a passport system implemented in Georgia, which previously lacked one. Railroaders and citizens increased their vigilance. Anyone appearing the least bit suspicious was in for a tough round of questioning.

In the end, the ultimate loss was eight good men to the noose.

CONCLUSION

Overall, Andrews developed a good plan, collected adequate intelligence, and anticipated many situations and needs. This was in an era when "raids" were quick hit-and-run forays to create as much destruction and confusion as possible to harass local forces. Few had strategic implications. Andrews had no previous examples or "doctrine" as guidelines or lessons to learn from. He developed the plan based solely on his year or so of experience as a line-crosser and his instincts. Nothing comparable had ever been attempted before, and very little has been since.

Regardless of the errors, flaws, and uncontrollable events foiling the raid, what it really comes down to is one individual: William Fuller. The determined and persistent conductor simply never gave up. There is little doubt that his unrelenting pursuit was the reason for the mission's failure. If another conductor had been on duty on the morning run north Andrews most likely would have succeeded.

A number of the participants and surviving raiders published memoirs. They tend to embellish and even fabricate parts of their stories. It is not uncommon for incorrect or conflicting events to be related. Some of the participants conducted ongoing feuds to the end of their days, accusing others of inflating their actions or diminishing the roles of others.

Besides numerous histories and memoirs by participants, two movies based on the Andrews' raid have been produced. Buster Keaton co-directed and starred in *The General*, a 1927 silent film very loosely based on the chase. While essentially a romantic comedy, it is worth viewing by those interested in the chase. The most notable movie was the 1956 Walt Disney production *The Great Locomotive Chase*, which was probably as responsible for promoting the story of the chase as any book. While there are inaccuracies—compression of events, gunplay, dramatically burning a boxcar on a bridge, and especially with the portrayal of the escape being much fictionalized—it does successfully portray the ambience of the dramatic chase.

Today the *General* is on display in Kennesaw, Georgia and the *Texas* is in Atlanta. The old W&A line is still owned by the State of Georgia and leased to CSX Transportation. Much of it remains a single-track route and mostly follows the original course. With patience and attention to detail one can follow the entire route on Google Earth and see many of the old landmarks.

One wishing to drive the route can follow a guide available in local museums or online. Virtually every notable site on the route is identified by historical markers and many of the old W&A railroad stations are now local museums recording the history of the Great Locomotive Chase. Graves of many of the participants are found in the Chattanooga National Cemetery and Atlanta's Oakland Cemetery.

Top: The locomotive Texas in 1911 before being placed in the Cyclorama Building in Atlanta's Grant Park. By this time it had been modified as a coal burner, had slightly smaller main driver wheels and a "thinner" stack, and lost its V-shaped cowcatcher. (Bogle)

Bottom: A memorial, complete with a bronze replica of the *General*, commemorating the Andrews' raiders overlooks the executed raiders' graves, to include James Andrews', in the Chattanooga National Cemetery. The escaped and exchanged raiders' names are listed on the ends of the monument. (Allen Shoppe)

GLOSSARY

abutment The part of a bridge that supports a great deal of weight or pressure.

audacious Daring or reckless.

barricade An obstruction that is used to block the passage of an enemy.

boxcar A railroad car that is enclosed and used to carry freight.

bushwhacker A type of guerrilla warfare used during the Revolutionary War and Civil War where groups of ordinary citizens would perpetrate raids on opposing forces.

caisson A watertight chamber used in construction work that is to be done underwater.

casualty A victim, usually in a military situation, who is killed or injured.

civilian An individual who is not in the military.

conductor A railway employee who is in charge of managing freight, passengers, and other employees.

crosstie A cross brace that support the rails on a railway track; also called a railroad tie.

guerilla A type of warfare in which small groups of combatants use military tactics to harass or sabotage a larger force.

handcar A railroad car powered by its passengers, or by people pushing the car from behind.

infantry Soldiers specifically trained to fight on foot.

locomotive A rail vehicle that provides the power to move a train.

quinine A crystalline alkaloid made from cinchona bark that is used as a medicine.

regiment A military unit usually consisting of a number of battalions.

saboteur An individual who perpetrates a deliberate action against an enemy aimed at weakening the opposing force through subversion, obstruction, disruption, or destruction.

secessionist A person who supported the South withdrawing from the Union.

telegraph A outdated communication system that was used to transmit messages in Morse Code over electrical wires.

unorthodox Contrary to what is usual, traditional, or accepted.

warfare Military operations between enemies.

FOR MORE INFORMATION

Abraham Lincoln Presidential Library
112 North 6th Street
Springfield, IL 62701
(217) 558-8844
Web site: http://www.alplm.org/home.html
A public, non-circulating research library that contains material on all aspects of Illinois history.

American Civil War Museum
297 Steinwehr Avenue
Gettysburg, PA 17325
(717) 334-6245
Web site: http://www.gettysburgmuseum.com
Wax museum with more than 35 scenes and over 300 life-sized wax figures representing key moments of the Civil War.

Lincoln Museum
66 Lincoln Square
Hodgenville, KY 42748
(270) 358-3163
E-mail: abe@lincolnmuseum-ky.org
Web site: http://www.lincolnmuseum-ky.org/Index.html
Collection of artifacts in Abraham Lincoln's birth state.

National Civil War Museum
One Lincoln Circle at Reservoir Park
Harrisburg, PA 17103
(717) 260-1861
Web site: http://www.nationalcivilwarmuseum.org
A museum with a collection of artifacts, manuscripts, documents, and photographs presenting both sides of the conflict without bias.

Tennessee Valley Railroad Museum
4119 Valley Railroad Museum
Chattanooga, TN 37421
(423) 894-8028
Web site: http://www.tvrail.com
Rail museum that features rail trips in Tennessee.

Texas Civil War Museum
760 Jim Wright Freeway North
Fort Worth, TX 76108
(817) 246-3951

Web site: http://texascivilwarmuseum.com/index.html
A privately owned and funded collection of artifacts with over 15,000 square feet of exhibits.

Web Sites

Due to the changing nature of Internet links, Rosen Publishing has developed an online list of Web sites related to the subject of this book. This site is updated regularly. Please use this link to access the list:

http:// www.rosenlinks.com/raid/loco

FOR FURTHER READING

Aiken, Gene, *The Great Locomotive Chase as Told by the Men Who Made It Happen*, Historic Press/South, Gatlinburg, TN (1994)

Bonds, Russell S., *Stealing the General: The Great Locomotive Chase and the First Medal of Honor*, Westholme Publishing, Yardly, PA (2007)

Cohen, Stan & Bogle, James G., *The General & the Texas: A Pictorial History of the Andrews Raid, April 12, 1862,* Pictorial Histories Publishing, Missoula, MT (1999)

Jones, Robert C., *Retracing the Route of the General*, Bartow History Center, Casterville, GA (1996)

O'Neill, Charles, *Wild Train: The Story of the Andrews Raiders*, Random House, New York (1956)

Pittenger, William, *Daring and Suffering: A History of the Great Railroad Adventure*, J.W. Daughaday, Philadelphia (1863)

Pittenger, William, *Capturing a Locomotive: A History of Secret Service in the Late War,* National Tribune, Washington, DC (1884)

Pittenger, William, *Daring and Suffering: A History of the Andrews Railroad Raid*, War Publishing Company, New York (1887)

Scaife, William R., *Joe Brown's Pets: The Georgia Militia, 1862–1865*, Mercer University Press, Macon, GA (2004)

Wilson, John A., *Adventures of Alf Wilson: A Thrilling Episode*, National Tribune, Washington, DC (1880)

INDEX

ABOUT THE AUTHOR

Gordon L. Rottman entered the U.S. Army in 1967, volunteered for Special Forces, and completed training as a weapons specialist. He served in the 5th Special Forces Group in Vietnam in 1960–70 and subsequently in airborne infantry, long-range patrol and intelligence assignments until retiring after 26 years. He was a Special Operations Forces scenario writer at the Joint Readiness Training Center for 12 years and is now a writer, living in Texas.